YOUR CHILD
AT PLAY

One to Two Years

YOUR CHILD AT PLAY:

One to Two Years

Exploring, Learning, Making Friends, and Pretending

SECOND EDITION

MARILYN SEGAL, PH.D.

Foreword by WENDY MASI, PH.D.,
Director of the Family Center at Nova Southeastern University

A "Your Child at Play" Series Book

NEWMARKET PRESS   NEW YORK

To my parents, for their optimism and hope

The author gratefully acknowledges the continuing grant from the A.L. Mailman Family Foundation, Inc., which supported the writing of this book.

All royalties earned on the sales of Your Child at Play *books are contributed to the Family Center of Nova Southeastern University.*

Drawn from research conducted at The Family Center, Nova Southeastern University, Ft. Lauderdale, Florida.

SECOND EDITION

10   9   8   7   6   5

Library of Congress Cataloging-in-Publication Data:

Segal, Marilyn M.
    Your child at play. One to two years / Marilyn Segal.—2nd ed.
       p.   cm.
    Includes index.
    ISBN 1-55704-335-3 (hardcover). —ISBN 1-55704-331-0 (pbk.)
    1. Child rearing.   2. Child development.   3. Play.   4. Learning
    5. Creative activities and seat work.   I. Title
    HQ767.9.S425   1998
    649'.122—DC21   97-48598
                                                                CIP

QUANTITY PURCHASES
Companies, professional groups, clubs, and other organizations may qualify for special terms when ordering quantities of this title. For information, write to Special Sales, Newmarket Press, 18 East 48th Street, New York, NY 10017; call (212) 832-3575; or fax (212) 832-3629.

PHOTO CREDITS
LISA NALVEN PHOTOGRAPHY: pages 1, 3, 6, 8, 10, 16, 18, 20, 22, 23, 24, 25, 28, 29, 30, 31, 36 top, 39, 40, 44 left, 45 right, 50, 55, 56, 57, 61, 62 bottom, 65, 66, 69, 71, 73, 74, 77, 78, 81, 86 bottom left, 84, 85, 86, 90, 92, 94, 106, 109, 110, 113, 114, 115, 118 bottom, 124, 125, 127 bottom, 129, 132, 137, 140, 144, 146, 154, 157, 160, 163 bottom left, 170, 173, 180, 183, 184, 188, 190, 197, 201, 210, 215, 217, 223 left, 225, 226, 231, 233, 236, 238, 239, 240, 242, 244, 249, 253 bottom, 255 right, 257, 259, 260, 263, 264, 266, 267 right, 273, 274, 275, 276 right, 284.
BILL SARCHET: pages 12, 17, 19, 21, 32, 36 bottom, 37, 41, 42, 44 right, 45 left, 46, 47, 48, 52, 53, 58, 59, 60, 62 top, 63, 67, 68, 70, 75, 86 top right, 86 top left, 86 bottom right, 83, 87, 95, 100, 101 bottom, 103, 107, 108, 116, 117, 118 top, 119, 120, 121, 127 top, 130, 135, 136, 138, 141, 152, 155, 163 top left and right, 163 bottom right, 164, 165, 167, 172, 176, 179, 191, 195, 198, 202, 203, 204, 206, 209, 212, 213, 221, 223 right, 228, 229, 232, 234, 235, 246, 247, 248, 253 top right, 254, 255 left, 258, 267 left, 278, 281, 283.

Book design by M.J. DiMassi
Manufactured in the United States of America.

Acknowledgments

~~~~~~

This book is a collaborative effort.

WENDY MASI, Ph.D., Director of the Family Center at Nova Southeastern University, is my toughest critic. She raked through the manuscript with a fine-tooth comb and weeded out passages that were inaccurate or unclear. Dr. Masi has three delightful children of her own, who just happen to be my grandchildren.

RONI LEIDERMAN, Ph.D., Director of Nova Southeastern University's Family Institute, has years of intimate experience with families of very young children. She and her staff tried out all the suggested activities with parents and babies, and helped me make appropriate changes. She identified cooperative families with adorable children to participate in our photo sessions.

ANN MCELWAIN, M.B.A., Director of Marketing and Product Development at the Family Center at Nova Southeastern University, assumed the major responsibility for implementing the photo sessions. She has an uncanny way of convincing babies to do the right thing at the right time.

SUZANNE GREGORY, my most valuable assistant, has the talent to decipher my handwriting and incorporate volumes of new material and rewrites into a manageable manuscript.

Foreword

~~~~~~

Your Child at Play is a series of books about the joy of playing with your child. When you and your child play together, you are enhancing your child's creativity and imagination, and encouraging flexible thinking. You are also getting back in touch with your own childhood, discovering a playful part of yourself that may have been buried through the years. But most important, you're connecting with your child. You are creating a bond of intimacy that will keep you and your child together in spirit, even through the often stormy teenage years.

The author of this series, Marilyn Segal, is an expert in child development, a noted professor, author, lecturer, researcher, and the founder of Nova Southeastern University's Family Center in Ft. Lauderdale, Florida, devoted to strengthening the family and enhancing the ability of parents and caregivers to nurture children. She is also a mother and grandmother whose heart and soul is invested in children, and believes more than anything in the power of play. Her home is filled with blocks, trains, books, crafts, and dolls, carefully selected so that they will be loved by all her children. Her grandchildren spend hours playing with her dollhouse and Brio set, weaving magical special worlds to which only they and their Nana are privy.

This book series is special because their author is special. She is a five-foot, ninety-pound powerhouse, who believes that everyone should experience the joy of play, and that playing together is at the heart of every relationship. She is my mother, my mentor, my friend. Her simple message "play together, grow together" is as powerful as it is succinct. Enjoy the books, follow your heart, and you will all have fun.

—Wendi Masi, Ph.D., Director of the Family Center
at Nova Southeastern University

~~~

Contents

First Thoughts

Nicholas, twenty months, was sitting on his cousin's tricycle protesting loudly because the pedals would not turn. When his Dad leaned over to give him a helpful push, his protests grew even louder. Nicholas did not want help with this tricycle. He wanted to ride it himself.

Taking care of a child between one and two years old is an exciting experience. The toddler year is a period of self-definition. Children, like Nicholas, discover that they are distinct individuals with the ability to manage things on their own and make other people do their bidding. As they explore their own capabilities, they are bound to meet frustration. Upset and out of sorts, they inevitably send mixed messages to the adults around them. "Leave me alone. I can do it myself!" "Help. I'm having trouble!"

One to Two Years is a practical guide for parents who are faced with the everyday challenges of living with a toddler. Each section of *One to Two Years* focuses on a different topic or issue familiar to parents of one-year-olds: "Explorations," "Everyday Living," "Making Connections," and "Having Fun." A major theme that emerges is the competing objectives parents have to juggle during the second year. How can you encourage independence and still help children accept reasonable limits and follow rules? How can you take advantage of your child's ability to learn without creating pressure or taking the fun out of play? Despite our practical orientation, we do not offer precise solutions to such dilemmas. Striking a balance between competing objectives, which is the rule rather than the exception, is ultimately up to you.

It is our firm belief that there is no one best way to parent a toddler. One-year-olds flourish in many different family settings with different styles of care giving. In *One to Two Years* we describe a range of alternatives so that you, as a parent, can follow the suggestions and try out the play ideas that seem right for your family.

EXPLORATION

Introduction

~~~~~~

Mother (looking into a baby carriage as she holds her toddler by the hand): "What
an adorable baby! What beautiful big blue eyes! Terry, see the pretty baby!"
Terry (reaching into the carriage and poking at the baby's face): "Eyes—baby eyes."
Mother: "Be gentle Terry. Just touch the baby's hand. We don't want to hurt the
baby."

As a parent of a one-year-old, you can relate to this scene. There is a big difference between taking care of a baby and taking care of a toddler. In the first year of life, you are concerned with understanding your baby's cues and meeting your baby's needs. Beginning in the second year, you change your focus. You are concerned with helping your toddler become more self-sufficient and responsible. You are no longer satisfied with doing everything for your child. Instead, you encourage her to explore her surroundings and discover her own capacities.

It has been said time and again that you have to be young to be a parent. This saying really strikes home in the toddler years. From morning to night, the typical toddler is on the go and into everything in sight. On the positive side, your child is a great companion—enthusiastic, vital, and excited by each new discovery. On the problem side, your energetic and curious youngster requires constant watching. Just as toddlers, in time, will learn the rules about which are okay and not okay explorations, parents, in time, learn strategies for limiting unsafe explorations without resorting to a "no." While an occasional "no" won't hurt your toddler, too many "no's" discourage exploration and reduce opportunities to learn.

The first section of this book is devoted to issues related to exploration. In Chapter 1, Hands on Everything, we discuss how you can respond to your toddler's desire to handle all kinds of objects. In Chapter 2, Emptying and Filling, we look at how you can guide your toddler through the stage of emptying and filling containers and rearranging the house. In Chapter 3, Gaining Physical Prowess, we describe how you can both encourage and protect your child as she practices new physical skills. Throughout these three chapters, there is a common theme: ways to encourage exploration while still keeping it within bounds.

CHAPTER 1

Hands on Everything

The Scene: *The living room in Grandma's house.*

Mother: *"Now that this granddaughter of yours has learned to walk, she's into everything."*

Grandma: *"It's okay. There's not a thing in here she could break. Just put her down and let her play."*

A few seconds later:

Mother: *"Oh dear, Amelia just pulled on the tablecloth and knocked that flower vase on the floor."*

Grandma: *"Mmm—oh, well. It wasn't that valuable anyway." (Smiling and holding Amelia in the air.) "You are a little lightening bolt, aren't you? I'm just glad that you didn't get hurt. Now, let's see if we can find some toys for you."*

Toddlers are well-known for the delight they take in investigating objects. The most interesting objects, of course, are those that are off limits: a row of perfume bottles, a delicate china figurine, a newly acquired CD player. While some toddlers are content with a cursory examination, most toddlers feel compelled to try out the perfumes, pick up the figurine, or turn every knob on the stereo.

Even toddlers who are usually satisfied with a cursory examination can be intrigued by a particularly interesting object. Predictably, the end result is a crash. No matter how much a parent supports exploration, or how trustworthy the toddler is, sooner or later all parents of toddlers have to establish rules that limit exploration.

From the point of view of your toddler, guidelines for touching or not touching objects are rather complicated. Some objects can never be touched, some objects can be touched all the time, and some objects can be touched only when a grown-up is around to supervise. Objects that appear to be similar have to be treated differently. A wind-up musical toy can be treated roughly, but Grandma's antique music box cannot be picked up at all. The string of beads from Mother's top drawer can be dragged around the house, but the beads that she keeps in her jewelry box are permanently off limits. Picking the leaves off house plants is forbidden, but pulling weeds out of the garden is a way of being helpful. It is understandable that toddlers need a good measure of time and guidance in order to discriminate between these different situations.

RULES ABOUT TOUCHING

In most homes, parents keep dangerous objects such as sharp knives, medicines, and detergents out of a toddler's reach. But even in the best child-proofed homes, there are many "don't touch" objects. In the bathroom, for example, the toilet bowl is a major attraction. In the kitchen, there is a refrigerator and a garbage container. In the living room, there are expensive stereo systems, delicate china, and valuable books.

At first, you may try to keep your toddlers away from forbidden objects by closing doors or putting up barriers. This technique has limitations. Keeping the door closed is effective with a room that is seldom used, such as your bedroom. But when the door is frequently opened and closed, toddlers become aware of their parent's strategy and work hard to beat the system. As Brian's mother put it, "My son has a sixth sense. The one time out of a hundred I forget to close that bathroom door, he's in there splashing in the toilet."

After a while, you may decide that it is easier to teach your toddler some "don't touch" rules than to spend the day playing guard. One of the simplest ways to keep a child from handling off-limit objects is to provide alternatives. Anton's father told us his son was into everything: the silverware drawer in the kitchen, the CD cabinet in the living room, and the linen closet in the bathroom. In the kitchen, the problem was at least partially solved by setting aside two drawers for Anton. In the living room, a lower shelf was reserved for objects that were safe to handle. Even in the bathroom, unrestricted exploration was allowed in one small drawer.

Parents who use the special drawer strategy suggest that rather than placing toys in the child's drawer or cabinet, you put in adult objects. In the kitchen cabinet, for instance, put a couple of pots with lids, a sponge, a wooden spoon, a set of measuring cups, and a strainer. In the family room, fill a desk drawer with junk mail, old magazines, and an outdated TV listing. Then change these adult objects on a regular basis, removing items that are no longer of interest and substituting new ones that pose a greater challenge.

No matter how clever you are in providing substitute objects or diverting explorations, there will be times when your toddler discovers objects that are off limits. In these situations the most effective restraint is a verbal message. Children are sensitive to tone of voice and will respond to a single word like "hot," "sharp," or "dirty." At twenty-two months, Allison had learned that she couldn't have a sip of coffee because it was too hot. When a guest came over and was served coffee, Allison spoke to her sternly as she was about to take a sip, "No-no, hot!" Although toddlers may not always know when to apply a rule, the one word message, if not used too often, can be an effective restraint.

As your toddler's understanding of language grows, words can be used to tell her what she can do as well as what she cannot do. Instead of saying no, or don't touch, you may want to use words like "touch gently," "make nice," "let's carry it together," or "we have to be careful."

Tina's mother took advantage of the fact that Tina liked to point at objects. She taught Tina how to touch delicate objects with an extended forefinger, as if she were pointing at them. Soon Tina understood that the phrase "just touch" meant that her exploration was limited to this special kind of pointing. David's father used a similar verbal prompt with his son, who kept trying to stick his fingers into their dachshund's eyes. "Make nice, Corky," he explained, as he showed his son how to pat the dog softly on the head.

A logical extension of "touch gently" is "hold it carefully." Having identified the fact that certain objects require special handling, a toddler is ready to take on the greater challenge of holding a delicate object. At first you will want to show your child how to hold the object while standing still. After a while, your child will learn to carry an object from one spot to the

next, putting it down very gently. Parents who have not risked this kind of teaching are often surprised at how trustworthy toddlers are when they are given the opportunity to learn.

When teaching your child how to handle objects carefully, it is especially important to phrase explanations in a positive way. Rather than saying, "Be careful not to rip the pages," you can say to your child, "Turn the pages gently. It is such a pretty book." Rather than saying, "Don't crush the flower," you can say, "Touch the flower with your finger. It is very delicate." Finding verbal explanations that are simple enough to be understood is not easy, of course, but it is well worth the effort. With every explanation, you stimulate language development as you help your child learn safe ways of exploring.

WASTING THINGS

The toddler's tendency to get into everything creates problems for even the most relaxed parent. In addition to breaking things that are valuable, toddlers are notorious for wasting things. Crayon marks can appear on every page of a new pad of paper, a whole box of tissues can be scattered on the floor, or all the water can be poured out of the water cooler.

Toddlers have difficulty understanding words like "take just one tissue," or "squeeze out a little bit of toothpaste." When Justin's mother became upset over his over-zealous squeezing of the toothpaste tube, she said in a firm voice, "Don't squeeze out the whole tube, just use a little." Justin dutifully squeezed out just a little bit of toothpaste. But when his mother took the toothpaste away, Justin began to complain. "Need more a little bit," he insisted in a cross between a whine and a snort.

Because toddlers are unlikely to understand either ecology or economy, the best way to handle waste is to give toddlers limited supplies: three tissues rather than a box, sheets of toilet paper rather than a roll, a few pieces of paper rather than a pad. While this strategy will not eliminate the "need more a little bit," it does put some limits on the toddler's tendency to waste.

Keeping the house in order is another challenge associated with a toddler's need for hands-on explorations. Unquestionably, toddlers and parents have different ideas about where things go. Your toddler may figure out how to open drawers and redistribute their contents, or how to take the feathers out of a pillow. Because toddlers see nothing inappropriate about their rearrangements, your best resort is a watchful eye.

Much more serious than making a mess is getting into things that are dangerous. Somehow or other, toddlers have a way of finding a sharp knife, a bag of fertilizer, or a bottle of cleaning fluid that has accidentally been left out. Toddler-proofing a house or yard is a never-ending challenge.

Whether the problem is breakage, waste, mess, or danger, a toddler's hands-on exploration is troublesome. During the first year, you spent a good deal of time nurturing and soothing your baby. Quite suddenly you find yourself assuming the role of watchdog. Your challenge is to keep the house and your child intact without restricting the urge to explore or using a punitive approach.

In this chapter, we have discussed some danger control strategies. Unquestionably, the most effective strategy is to help your child learn rules about exploration. Once your toddler has learned some "hand-on, hands-off" rules, you will see explorations in a more positive light. As children poke and prod, pick up and examine, carry and transfer, arrange and rearrange, they are learning about the properties of objects. Differences in size, weight, texture, and durability are discovered. Although we may not think about it when we mend a piece of broken china, the explorations of the toddler provide basic insights that are essential for future learning.

PLAY IDEAS

Whether your toddler is twelve months or twenty-four months old, timid or fearless, most of her waking hours are devoted to explorations. This means, of course, that you find yourself constantly on your guard. Is there a door she can slam on her hands, an electric cord she can pull, a high place she can fall off of, a bureau that could topple over on her, some medicine or cleaning fluid that she could somehow get her hands on? Without negating the importance of keeping close watch on your toddler, we suggest ideas that encourage safe exploration.

As you choose activities for your toddler, take into account her personality and preferences. Some children are energetic and intrepid explorers who get into everything, open and close every drawer in sight, pull every book out of the bookcase, and make a grand mess. Other toddlers are timid explorers who are bothered by new sensations like paste on their fingers or sand between their toes, or frightened by bright lights, loud noises, and unfamiliar sights.

Our Play Ideas suggests ways of keeping your toddler productively occupied by providing her with a collection of interesting toys and objects, and engaging her in activities that support her need to explore.

Making Things Work

An exciting experience for all toddlers is the discovery that they can make things happen. As you search for manipulable toys, make sure to think about not only what the toy can do, but what your child can do with the toy.

Latch Boards

The latches that fascinate one-year-olds as they explore cupboards, closets, and window frames can be duplicated on a latch board. If the latches are hinged in some way when they are attached to the board, the manipulable play is even more fun. After all, when something is unlatched it should swing open.

Pop-up Toys

Pop-up toys are standard equipment in toddlers' toy collections. Pushing down levers and twisting knobs are great ways for children to practice fine motor skills. More important, as children push the right lever or turn the right knob, they develop a real sense of accomplishment. "I can master this toy! I can make things happen!"

Flashlights

Toddlers enjoy turning a flashlight on and off, and they are curious about the way the beam of light touches other objects. Encourage your child to start with flashlight experiments in a well-lit

room and then progress gradually to dimmer surroundings. A lively light in a dark room can be a mysterious phenomenon.

Radios

A battery operated radio is another good toy. The knobs represent an interesting problem to be solved. One knob changes the volume, while the other changes the quality of the sound.

Pop Beads

Even a very young toddler can have fun with pop beads. At first your toddler will discover how to take them apart. After a while she will discover how to put them back together.

Toys and Activities That Encourage Sorting and Rearranging

Junk Mail

Interesting pictures arrive at your home every day in the form of junk mail. Let your child help open these envelopes. The mail also brings greeting cards, which are durable pictures just the right size for one-year-olds to handle and carry around.

Basket of Odds and Ends

Create a basket of odds and ends where your child is really free to get her hands on everything. The hardware store or a junk drawer is a good place to look for things with peculiar shapes or feels, objects that come apart and go together, unidentifiable objects that look like they serve a very useful purpose. Possible

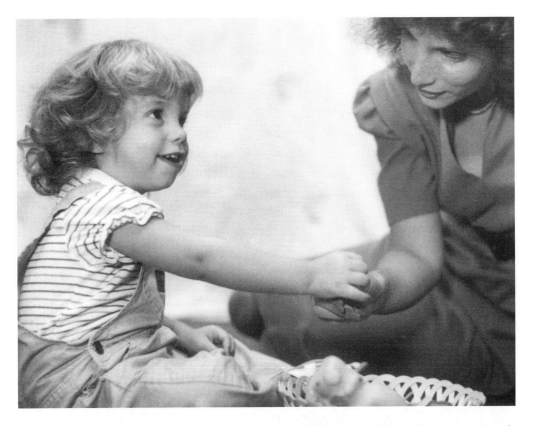

items for the basket are key rings, empty film canisters, a hand-kerchief, a bathtub plug, a clothespin, a broken zipper, a luggage tag, and a checkbook cover.

Reading Materials

One-year-olds are attracted to reading materials that they see adults handle. Many of these magazines and catalogs have thin pages that tear accidentally when children play with them. Give your child copies that you have already read, and then count on some damage. If your one-year-old starts tearing the pages intentionally, put the magazine or catalog away for a while and substitute a paper product that may be torn, such as used envelopes or napkins.

Photographs

Photographs of family members are intriguing to one-year-olds, but often must be handled with care. Try giving your child a few photographs that he can explore on his own. Slip pictures inside a clear plastic frame, or make a refrigerator toy by laminating the photograph and mounting a magnetic strip on the back. Still another possibility is to put several pictures in a pocket-size photo album and tape the sides of the pages so that the photographs can't be removed.

Cardboard Building Blocks

While wooden blocks can be turned too easily into throwing toys, cardboard blocks are both safe and intriguing. They can be stacked, nested, or arranged in a row. When they are turned around or upside down, a different picture appears.

Zoo and Farm Animals

Since toddlers are fascinated by animals, a collection of small rubber zoo animals invites sustained play. A favorite activity is standing up the animals and making them walk. Another activity is making a pile of animals that belong together. Don't expect your toddler to separate farm animals from zoo animals, or animals that walk from animals that fly. Your toddler is likely to have her own ideas about which animals belong together.

Measuring Cups

Give your child a set of measuring cups. As she experiments with different ways of playing with them, you may see her line them in a row, nest them, or turn them over and bang them with a spoon. Add another element of fun by giving her a small bowl of ice cubes. She will enjoy putting an ice cube in each cup.

Gentle Touching of Valuable Objects

Flower Show

Toddlers are attracted to flowers in a garden and may experiment with pulling off the petals or tearing off the leaves. Show

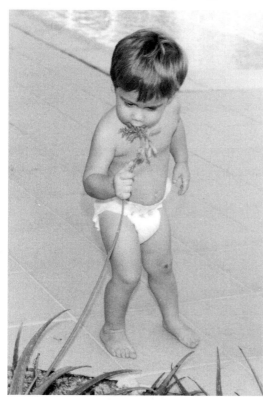

your toddler how to touch flowers very gently. With your help your toddler can learn that flowers need to be touched very gently, but it is all right to pick grass or pull out a weed. Make sure that no grass or weeds find their way into your toddler's mouth.

Fruit Picking

Picking fruit is a wonderful activity for a toddler as long as the fruit is hardy. Look for an opportunity to let your toddler help you harvest. Trees such as crab apple, orange, lemon, or lime can withstand a tug from a toddler.

CHAPTER 2

Emptying and Filling

The Scene: Aunt Minna is visiting her nephew, Karl, age sixteen months.

Aunt Minna: "Karl, let's put your toys back in the toy basket. Your room looks like a cyclone hit it. Aunt Minna will help."

Karl: "Minna!"

Aunt Minna: "Yes, I'm Aunt Minna. You know my name. Now, let's start with your stuffed animals. Come on Teddy, into the basket you go."

Five minutes later . . .

Aunt Minna: "All clean. You're such a big help!"

Karl: "All clean." (At this point, Karl picks up the basket and dumps the toys back on the floor.)

Although emptying and filling are two sides of the same coin, it is emptying, not filling, that most appeals to your one-year-old. If he has not already discovered the excitement of emptying by his first birthday, he soon will. And for the next few months, emptying behaviors of all kinds will appear. Book-shelves may be cleared, wastebaskets upended, toy boxes emptied of their contents. The rule seems to be "find a container, any container, and dump it."

It is logical to dump a container in order to see what is inside or to find a lost toy. Often, however, a toddler has a different goal in mind. Dumping is something to do for the fun of it. Emptying a purse, overturning the dog dish, spilling a box of blueberries onto the floor—this is a one- year-old's definition of having a good time.

Why are one-year-olds so entranced with emptying? A possible explanation is that emptying produces dramatic transformations. A composite object like a bookshelf comes apart into many different pieces when the books are removed. The

contents of a wastebasket assume a different shape when they are scattered on the floor. The relationship between container and contained, and the variety of possible transformations, are familiar matters to adults. But to one-year-olds, these changes are a source of wonderment and a reason for investigation.

Actually, emptying is just the most noticeable of the transformations that intrigue one-year-olds. Toddlers also like to move objects from one location to another, perhaps amassing a collection in an unusual spot—under the couch, behind the bookshelf, or in the dirty clothes hamper. Sometimes they intentionally experiment with rearrangements, piling several objects on top of each other or lining them up in a row. Most often, they simply misplace objects by carrying them around for a while and then setting them down somewhere else.

KEEPING ORDER IN THE HOUSE

From a parent's point of view, all this emptying and rearranging behavior on the part of their one-year-old tends to have a common consequence: things around the house are no longer in their customary places, and the house looks messy. You find yourself seeking ways to limit emptying, even if your housekeeping standards are rather relaxed. An initial step that works for many parents is to alter the physical environment. Parents discourage emptying of wastebaskets by hiding them behind heavy pieces of furniture. They put enticing containers on high shelves or change the location of the dog's dish so that it is less accessible. In general, they reduce the total number of objects that are within reach of the child. One or two magazines on a table become less tempting than a full magazine rack. A few towels in a bathroom linen closet provoke less emptying than a closet full. A shelf or cupboard with a small number of toys can be kept intact more easily than a toy box filled to the brim.

As your toddler grows older, you will find yourself relying on verbal directives and explanations to limit messy exploration. Gradually your toddler will learn which emptying activities are unacceptable and which forms will be tolerated to a point. In the process, he will also become aware that emptying is a powerful way to gain attention from adults. For a period of time, emptying is a cat and mouse game in which toddlers intentionally violate the rules. They may empty flowerpots by digging out the dirt, or unzip the couch cushions and remove the stuffing that is inside. If you are quick to clean up such messes, your toddler may be inspired to make an even bigger mess in order to watch you work harder.

It is natural for one-year-olds and parents to clash over messy exploration. Parents are concerned about maintaining order, while children are interested in emptying, transferring, and rearranging objects. If you make too much out of this difference, however, you invite a power struggle. Be patient. Within a few months your toddler will begin to respect the family rules concerning messy exploration.

CONSTRUCTIVE REARRANGEMENTS

Teaching and reinforcing workable limits for messy exploration is a reasonable goal. This goal is furthered when you encourage forms of exploration that promote order. Although many one-year-olds are fascinated with emptying, they are also attracted to filling. A twelve-month-old baby already enjoys dropping stones into a bucket, or stuffing cookies into a cup of juice. Between one and two years of age, this interest in filling steadily grows. Some filling experiments, such as stuffing socks into the toilet, can be just as troublesome as emptying behavior, but fill-

ing activities are generally constructive. Instead of taking things apart, children are putting things together, and they often help accomplish a family task.

Among the constructive filling jobs that toddlers manage at an early age are filling the wastebasket with paper and filling the hamper with laundry. Recognizing that such filling activities carry adult prestige, toddlers carry out these chores with great enthusiasm. Brian, at fourteen months, considered himself custodian of the vegetable bin. After each trip to the grocery store, he painstakingly lined up the onions on the bottom shelf of the bin. Benjamin became quite adept at arranging the canned food on the bottom shelf of the pantry. Many toddlers enjoy putting plastic cups into the dishwasher or clothes into the dryer.

One-year-olds can also be encouraged to pursue a variety of play activities that involve filling. Children generally fill a container in order to empty it, which means that the activity does not last unless a cycle is set up—filling, then emptying, filling, then emptying. This kind of cyclic play occurs easily enough with water and sand. It can also occur with substances such as rice, macaroni, or cereal-o's. Children are so intrigued by the process of pouring that they keep refilling their containers.

In order to establish the same kind of cycle with other play materials, there needs to be some special incentive for filling. Most often the factor that provides this extra incentive is an unusual container. An empty gallon milk jug is fun to fill with

small objects. Leftover shopping bags, or old purses that are easy to open, stimulate filling. Pockets of any kind on the clothes of one-year-olds are fascinating containers.

The attraction of filling is even greater when children become interested in transferring material from one container to another. In their water play, for example, older toddlers try to pour water from one cup to another. Once parents sense that their children are interested in the transfer idea, a second container can be introduced into a familiar routine.

If your toddler enjoys emptying a junk drawer in the kitchen, you might show him how to fill a toy shopping cart (or a shopping bag) with things from the drawer. Later, you could encourage him to transfer the items back to the junk drawer. If your toddler enjoys putting objects such as rocks or walnuts into a plastic bowl, add a second bowl with water in it. Muffin tins and egg cartons are particularly versatile. A handful of raisins or cereal-o's can be distributed again and again until they end up in someone's stomach.

Puzzle play is the most advanced form of filling for one-year-olds. Puzzles represent a category of containers in which the contents must be arranged in a precise manner. During the latter half of the second year, many children are able to complete very simple inset puzzles, but unless the insets are circles or squares, they are likely to need help. Your child may know where a piece belongs, but he does not know how to rotate the piece until it is perfectly in line with the hole.

When you help your one-year-old finish an inset puzzle, or fit plastic shapes into a shape sorter, he will experience an intense feeling of accomplishment. At the same time, however, this precise filling is potentially very frustrating. In fact, few things distress one-year-olds more than a puzzle that does not behave according to expectations.

Rather than frustrating your toddler with inset puzzles before he is ready, create your own puzzles out of simple containers. A hole big enough for a small block to pass through can be cut

in the lid of a coffee can, or a hole big enough for crayons can be cut in the top of a potato chip can. Containers like these are size sorters, easier to master than the shape sorters sold in toy stores. One-year-olds do not have to fill each hole with a particular shape, but they do have to pay attention to size.

Included in this intermediate territory of beginning puzzles is the case of the round peg in a round hole. Putting a round peg in a round hole offers one-year-olds the satisfaction of an inset puzzle without the accompanying frustration. Like an inset puzzle, the fit is precise, but there is no orientation problem. Large scale pegboards are traditional favorites. Another popular version of round pegs in round holes are miniature dolls that can be placed in furniture, cars, and other vehicles.

In reality, there are many intermediate points between the elementary task of filling a bucket with rocks and the demanding task of completing an inset puzzle. A whole range of containers are possible and each one helps children learn something about shape and size. A narrow-necked bottle cannot be filled with large objects; an envelope will not accommodate objects that are too thick; objects that are too long will stick out of a pocket. At first, putting the right piece in a puzzle is a matter of trial and error. As toddlers become more familiar with a puzzle, they are able to select the piece that fits before they put it in place.

"THINK BIG" AND "THINK SMALL" CHILDREN

When one-year-olds are playing with a pegboard, or with miniature dolls, one of their favorite activities is to stick their fingers in the holes. Filling this space with their fingers is one way to learn about spatial relationships. At the other extreme, some one-year-olds investigate spatial relationships by filling spaces with their whole bodies. They crawl into cupboards or giant boxes, climb into the clothes hamper, or squeeze between the wall and the bed frame.

The way one-year-olds use their own bodies to fill containers may reflect a certain style of manipulating play. Although all children handle and rearrange objects with their fingers, some children seem particularly fascinated with small scale exploration. Other children seem drawn to emptying and filling on a large scale. A child who thinks small will be attracted to different activities than a child who thinks big.

The "think small" child may be especially interested in squeezing the toothpaste out of the tube, fitting playing cards into a narrow box, or inserting keys into keyholes. The "think big" child is more likely to empty the bottom two shelves of the pantry or fill the hamper with a variety of clothes and toys. You can help your child develop constructive filling activities by keeping in mind these individual differences. If he enjoys playing with big things, you might buy a set of large nesting blocks, or a wagon for carting stones around the yard. If he is interested in small things, try miniature people that fit into vehicles, a wallet with play money, or an inset puzzle with knobs.

In this chapter, we have discussed a major form of manipulative play among one-year-old children—emptying and filling. Parents see the emptying first, and quite possibly they see too much of it. Their immediate reaction is to wonder how this emptying can be controlled. Most parents set limits that define certain messy forms of exploration as unacceptable. A more positive approach is to encourage constructive forms of exploration, especially filling. Encouraging one-year-olds to fill containers not only reduces emptying but also promotes the learning of new concepts.

For a long time, of course, emptying has the upper hand. Even after a period of play filling, or after a period of thoughtful rearranging, one-year-olds usually leave the materials in a cluttered state. There is a big difference, however, between an older toddler who leaves a mess after an extended play period and one who simply dumps a container and then walks away. Children who are learning to organize and fill as well as to empty are learning how to translate their curiosity about objects into sustained play.

PLAY IDEAS

It is natural for one-year-olds and parents to clash over messy exploration. Parents are concerned about maintaining order, while children are interested in emptying, transferring, and rearranging. If parents make too much of this difference, they invite a power struggle. One way to avoid confrontations is to set reasonable limits and then not overreact when your toddler goes beyond them. A second way to avoid confrontations is to provide your child with opportunities to empty and fill that do not make a mess.

Fill-It-Up Toys

Toddlers enjoy filling shape sorters, but if there are many different shapes, they probably will need a helping hand from Mom or Dad. Much simpler is a homemade sorting toy with only one hole through which your child can stuff a variety of objects. In this case, your job will be to take the lid off periodically and remove the contents so that your child can start all over again.

Pegboard

A pegboard with large pegs simulates a simple filling activity. Stacking toys serve the same purpose. You can make a homemade stacking toy with plastic lids and a spindle.

Recycled Containers

Familiar containers, like baby-wipe canisters, shampoo bottles, bandage boxes, and diaper boxes, hold special appeal for one-year-olds. When they are empty, give your child those plastic bottles and jars he has been trying to reach on the changing table or in the bathroom.

Milk Jugs

A gallon milk jug is an interesting container for filling, because the narrow neck is such a contrast to the spacious interior. Put some raisins inside a jug and let your one-year-old figure out how to pour them out.

Screw-On Lids

Your one-year-old probably likes containers with screw-on lids, although he may need help getting the lid on and off. Once the lid is off, he will be receptive to the idea of putting something inside before closing the container.

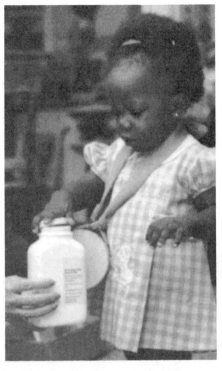

Purses

Purses are fun to investigate. Unfortunately, from a child's viewpoint, many purses are hard to open. Give your child a purse that stays open, or a tote bag, and encourage him to fill it. A purse can be filled with traditional items, such as hairbrushes, credit cards, tissues, play money, or old wallets. They can also be filled with unorthodox things such as balls, toy animals, and trucks. A long strap, which allows your child to carry the purse over his shoulder, will further increase its appeal.

Pocket Play

Buy or make a folder with pockets. Fill the pockets with colorful pictures or interesting objects such as straws or craft sticks. At first, your child will have fun pulling the items out of the pockets. After a while he might even try to put them back.

Gift Wrap

One-year-olds are learning about presents, those brightly decorated containers that arrive on holidays. You can create everyday presents for your child as well. One way is to wrap a favorite toy in a piece of mylar, put it on your child's plate at lunch or in his crib at naptime, and encourage him to unwrap it. Sing "Happy Birthday" as your child opens the present.

Filling Activities

Spooning

Filling is a natural activity in a sandbox because the larger the container that you fill, the more fun you get pouring the sand out. Try giving your one-year-old a large spoon or scoop to use as a tool for filling. Many children at this age are trying to learn how to use a spoon and fork at the table. Spooning up sand provides a good practice exercise, and spills are of no consequence.

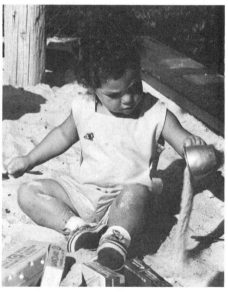

Pocket Search

Another natural filling activity is to put things in a pocket. Because many clothes for toddlers do not have pockets, children treat these accessories as luxuries. Consider making a smock or an apron with pockets for your child. "What's in your pocket today?" is a good conversation starter with a one-year-old who is lucky enough to have a pocket to fill.

Hose Play

Filling a container with water from a hose is a perennial favorite at all ages. Teach your one-year-old to fill outdoor flower pots or different sizes of tin cans and buckets with water. On occasion, they may fill a wading pool. The simplest approach is to show a one-year-old how to fill the depression at the base of a tree or shrub. Rarely can these plants be over-watered, and in a short while the water sinks into the ground, revealing once again a hole to be filled.

Scavenger Walk

Carry along a pail when taking a walk and collect small objects that interest you and your one-year-old. Soon your child will get the idea and start making his own contributions. He may even take over the job of carrying the container. Don't be surprised if he wants to dump the contents from time to time and begin again with a clean pail. Collected items are not necessarily meant to be kept at this age.

Scrapbooks

Filling a book makes sense to toddlers, as long as they can empty it at the same time. Photograph albums and scrapbooks, however, cannot take this kind of continuous reconstruction. You can create a satisfactory substitute with a blank photo album and a set of Colorform® characters. The Colorforms, which are thin plastic shapes, will stick to the plastic-coated pages of the album. Your child can endlessly move them from page to page with no damage to either the album or the Colorforms. If you want to give the pages more of a storybook look, put magazine pictures on the sticky surface inside the plastic covers. Then your child can place the Colorforms in different settings: a living room, a car, a mountain scene, a beach.

Little People

Fisher-Price® characters and similar miniature dolls are often sold with extensive playscapes such as airports, castles, and dollhouses. One-year-olds, however, are more interested in finding places to fit their "little people." If your one-year-old likes to handle these little dolls, try to buy accessories such as cars, buses, chairs, and toilets. Then your child will be able to fill and refill the holes with his newfound friends.

Kitchen Clean Up

The kitchen offers many opportunities for filling activities. Putting food away is one that does not overtax the skills of a toddler. With your help, a one-year-old may learn to remove specific items from the table every day and put them in the cupboard or the refrigerator. Stocking the kitchen after grocery shopping is even more exciting. Toddlers can put canned goods or cereal boxes in low cupboards, fill a crisper with vegetables that do not bruise easily, or arrange cheese and cold cuts in the proper compartment of the refrigerator.

Toy Bins

Rather than storing your child's toys in a single toy box or laundry basket, keep them in several smaller bins or baskets. The toys will be easier to find, and your child will be stimulated to transfer items from one basket to another.

Some for Me, Some for You

Small pieces of food, like cereal-o's or raisins, are especially good for filling games that involve transferring. Place two or more containers on a table, put the food in one of them, and show your child how to redistribute the food among the containers—a little here, a little there, and a little in your mouth.

Milk Carton and Blocks

Give your toddler a quart milk carton and a set of small wooden blocks. Let him practice dropping the blocks through the spout into the carton. At first you may have to help hold the carton steady as he drops the blocks in, but after a while he will learn to use one hand to hold the carton and the other hand to drop the block. He will also get increasingly more efficient at emptying the carton.

Tennis Ball Fun

Give your one-year-old a plastic tennis ball container and up to three tennis balls. Watch as he puts the balls in the container and then pours them out. Retrieving the runaway balls is half the fun of the game.

Nesting Cans

Give your toddler two or three empty cans of different sizes (make sure there are no sharp edges) and show him how to nest them. Even after he gets it right, he will take them apart and then try to get a larger one inside the smaller one. Don't be concerned about him regressing. He knows that the big one won't fit inside the little one, and he's trying to figure out why.

What's in My Pocket?

Hide a toy in your pocket. Let him reach in and get it out. He has learned that an object can be there even if you can't see it.

There's a Ball in My Pocket

Dress your toddler in an outfit that has pockets. Put a Ping-Pong or small rubber ball inside his pocket and see if he can get it out. Variations of this include putting a ball inside his sock, or putting small things in your own pocket and letting him transfer them into his.

Sorting the Mail

Save your junk mail. Your toddler will keep busy pulling the inserts out of the envelopes and trying to put them back. As you sort through the mail, give him one or two pieces and say, "This is your letter." If he get his own letters every day, he is apt to lose interest in yours.

Water Play

Water is a superior medium for transfer play. You can manage the dribbles and spills by setting up the activity outside. A variety of spoons, measuring cups, and metal bowls serve as non-breakable containers, and they make pleasant clinking sounds as the child plays. Try adding ice cubes to the water. They bob and float in the water, slither around in your child's hand or mouth, make a splash when poured, and eventually disappear altogether!

Shopping Play

Your toddler probably has a drawer or cupboard in the kitchen for exploration. Typically this place is emptied out day after day, and eventually your child grows bored. You can stimulate filling and rekindle interest in this junk drawer by introducing imaginary shopping. Armed with a shopping bag (or your 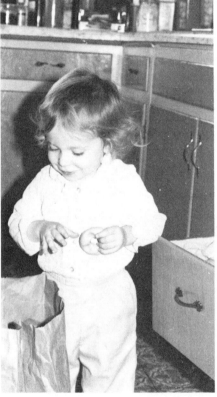 child's toy shopping cart), accompany your child to the drawer and pretend to purchase some of the items. Later in the day they can be dumped back in the drawer. If your child likes this way of playing, stock the drawer with objects that fit his shopping interests.

Keyholes

Keys are not only fun to play with because they are grown-up toys, but they also work well for a filling and emptying game. Put some old keys on a sturdy key ring and let your toddler go around the house in search of the keyholes. (Be sure all of your outlets are plugged, and that your child understands where keys go.)

For Those Who Think Big

Garbage Can

A large, plastic garbage can is an ideal toy for children who favor oversize containers. Even if your son can barely see over the top of the can, he will find a way to fill it with every imaginable sort of "garbage."

Playhouse

Children who think big like to get inside containers themselves. In fact, a large box may become a second home. You can extend this play by delivering things to the new address. "Knock, knock, here's some mail for you," you might announce as you hand him a book or a stuffed animal. In all likelihood, your child will respond by later carrying additional possessions to the new quarters.

Taking out the Trash

Putting trash in a wastebasket or garbage sack is fun for most toddlers. Children who want to go one step further can be encouraged to take a full receptacle to the outside garbage can and dump it in. Some trash may fall on the ground and your child will probably need help with the garbage can lid, but for a child who thinks big, this is a filling activity that is most gratifying.

CHAPTER 3

Gaining Physical Prowess

~~~~~~

The Scene: Two mothers with their children at a park.

First-time Mother: "Look at that. Your Jeffrey, he's standing up by himself! He's going to be walking any day now."

Jeff's Mother: "Yes, I suppose you're right."

First-time Mother: "Look, look at Jeff. He did it! He's walking by himself. He took four steps!"

Jeff's Mother: "It's exciting, isn't it? But now it means he's going to be harder to keep track of."

Experienced parents like Jeff's mother recognize that a child's first steps may be a mixed blessing. The excitement of seeing their baby develop such an important skill is tempered by the knowledge that walking ushers in a new era, one in which their baby will require greater supervision.

Whether they are early or late walkers, most children become accomplished walkers between the ages of one and two. Some children burst into walking, while others inch their way. Children who are on the heavy side, who are temperamentally cautious, or who focus their energies on other developmental tasks such as learning language are likely to be slow walkers. The normal limits for walking, however, are broad; they extend from eight to twenty months. As long as a youngster is within this normal range, the age at which walking begins tells us little about other facets of the child's intelligence.

Quite literally, walking brings with it a new world view. Growing a foot taller overnight makes the world look different,

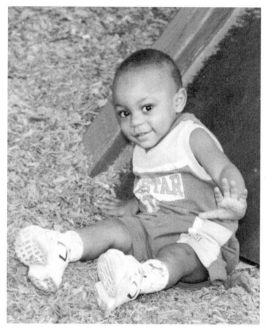

and getting around is different as well. Familiar patterns of movement must be relearned to mesh with walking. Turning around, sitting down, going under and over obstacles—all are changed when undertaken from a standing rather than a crawling position.

Parents often note that when one-year-olds gain control of walking, they look so much older. The act of walking does seem to give a child a sense of being grown-up, and with this sense comes an infusion of self confidence and vigor. There is a strong need to take on new chal-

lenges and discover new capabilities. In their excitement, children test themselves to the limit, struggling and straining to accomplish feats they see older people performing.

Frequently one-year-olds undertake more than they can manage and are frustrated. Why, you may wonder, does my child always have to do things the hard way? Why does she have to push the baby carriage through that narrow doorway? Why is she still climbing on the bed after just falling off? Like climbing a mountain because it is there, taking on new obstacles is a means of self definition for the one-year-old. "The more powerful I am physically," the child seems to be thinking, "the more significant I am as a person."

LIFTING AND CARRYING

In the initial stages, walking is a matter of using hands as well as feet. Babies pull themselves to a standing position and hold onto pieces of furniture in order to sidestep around a room. Even when babies no longer need to hold onto things for support, they often hold something in their hands as a source of security.

As your child becomes more adept at walking with her hands full, she will challenge herself to carry larger and heavier loads. A purse is replaced by a heavy briefcase; a small rubber ball by a big basketball. Typically parents respond to such achievements with words of praise. "Oh, you are a strong boy lifting that great big basketball!" "What a big girl to carry Daddy's briefcase!" Because they are proud of their one-year-old's new lifting ability, parents reinforce the connection between being grown-up and being physically powerful.

PUSHING AND PULLING

Another discovery that toddlers make once they have mastered walking is that objects can be pushed or pulled. Pushing actually facilitates walking because children can lean on the pushed object and, with practice, learn to look ahead and steer while they are pushing. Pulling, by contrast, is more difficult. Children need to look back and forth as they pull, first ahead to see what is coming, then behind to see how the pulled object is progressing. When toddlers discover pull toys, they are likely to go around the house searching for other objects to pull. However, once each pull toy is mastered, it tends to lose its appeal. The future lies with pushing, steering, and, ultimately, pretending to drive.

One of the most popular push toys is a popper, a kind of walking stick that makes music or creates an interesting visual display when it is pushed. However, one-year-olds can achieve

the same type of effect with less fanfare by pushing a broom, a mop, or even a tennis racket around the house. Alexis, at fourteen months, discovered an old guitar and came thumping down the hall, pushing it along like a hockey stick. What these household items lack in the way of fancy colors and unusual noises, they make up for in status by being adult objects.

Toys with wheels are even better for pushing. Toddlers continue to get on their hands and knees when they push miniature vehicles, but they also discover that walking gives them enough leverage to push larger vehicles. Grunting and groaning, toddlers are capable of maneuvering a surprising assortment of such objects: strollers, grocery carts, tricycles, wheelbarrows. Unfortunately, these vehicles often get stuck in tight spots or crash into obstacles.

You can avoid some problems by encouraging your child to become interested in smaller versions of vehicles. A toy shopping cart is more manageable than a grocery cart, a doll buggy (or doll stroller) is better than a regular stroller, a push-type riding toy is more satisfactory than a tricycle. As your child grows older, she will use her riding toy for going on a pretend trip, and her cart-type toy to go to the supermarket or take her doll for a stroll.

Problems sometimes arise as a one-year-old tries out a variety of pushing feats. Adam, at one year, had an absolute fetish about shutting doors. Despite his mother's fears, he was quite adept at keeping his fingers from getting pinched. However, Adam's door-shutting mania still created problems. As

soon as a door was shut, he wanted it open again. Finally, Adam's mother draped towels over the top of Adam's favorite doors so that they would not close completely when he tried to shut them.

Despite the occasional problems that occur, the pushing and pulling skills of one-year-olds find acceptable outlets. There are enough opportunities to practice without becoming destructive or endangering anyone. As was the case with lifting, parents and children are able to agree that this new form of muscle power is a sign of maturity.

THROWING, POUNDING, AND CLIMBING

Not all forms of one-year-old muscle power are as easily accommodated in everyday life. Between the ages of one and two, children learn to swing their arms forcefully and to direct the impact of this swinging motion in a particular direction at a particular spot. In plain words, they discover how to throw and to pound. One-year-olds who are just learning to throw and

pound are neither accurate nor selective. Any object is fair game in their opinion; if it makes a splat, a thud, or some other interesting sound, so much the better. One-year-olds are not bent on destruction when they throw and pound, but they are not very upset by it either.

When your one-year-old enthusiastically whacks a dinner plate with a spoon, or tosses food on the floor, you will clearly recognize the gulf that separates you from your toddler. From your child's point of view, throwing and pounding is a glorious display of power. From your perspective, however, throwing and pounding look like destructive behaviors that need to be restricted.

The most effective strategy for coping with pounding and throwing is redirection. The child who is pounding on a dinner plate can be redirected to a pounding bench or an xylophone. The child who is throwing food can be taken out of the high chair and given a ball to throw. Verbal prompts like "balls are

for throwing" may help with a child who is tuned into language. However, as opportunities to practice throwing and pounding are restricted, your toddler may lose some of her feelings of exhilaration. The feeling of accomplishment, which accompany any new physical skill, are diminished.

Much the same process occurs with another form of new muscle power—climbing. At first, climbing is primarily a means of getting onto adult pieces of furniture. Toddlers learn to climb onto adult-sized chairs, beds, and sofas. Most parents are pleased that their children are learning a new skill and encourage them to sit down when they reach the top. In time, however, one-year-olds climb higher and parents withdraw much of their support. Parents get increasingly upset as their children practice climbing on the kitchen counter, the dining table, and the dressers.

However, it would be misleading to exaggerate the conflicts over throwing, pounding, and climbing that take place between parents and one-year-olds. Families do find ways for one-year-olds to experiment with these new skills. In many homes, for example, various throwing games arise. A diaper may be tossed back and forth as part of a dressing routine, or dirty clothes may be thrown in the hamper. Rag dolls and stuffed animals have a tendency to leap from one family member to another.

Pounding, which has been directed toward a cobbler's bench or xylophone, can be extended to other objects under close supervision. Obviously, the blows of a one-year-old cannot harm such things as a carpet or the cushions on a couch. If you give your child a small rubber or plastic hammer, she can tap on floors, walls, non-breakable toys, and appliances without causing any real damage.

Greater climbing also can be allowed with parental supervision. Toddlers can be permitted to climb up and down carpeted stairs or practice climbing onto a sturdy armchair or sofa. Under the watchful eye of parents, children can climb up onto counters on specific occasions, such as climbing on the bathroom counter when it is time to brush their teeth. Climbing to a higher spot may be acceptable when the purpose is to watch something rather than to get into mischief. With you standing close by, your one-year-old might stand on a chair to watch you making a cake, to find the fish in the aquarium, or to look at the cars out the window.

Throwing, pounding, and climbing are far from forbidden activities in most homes. However, the fact remains that these new forms of muscle power are seldom freely exercised. Throwing soft materials or pounding with a toy hammer is better than no throwing or pounding, yet it is not quite the real thing. Feelings of mastery and potency are somewhat muted. Moreover, the limited number of opportunities to throw, pound, or climb

means that the rules for such exploration are complicated. How soft does something have to be before it can be thrown? How hard can something be hit without causing damage? How high is too high when climbing on the furniture?

While there is no simple way out of this quandary, finding a play environment in which throwing, pounding, and climbing are acceptable is a good compromise. Most parents discover that the best play environment for a physically active toddler is outdoors. Outside the house there are fewer valuables to break by throwing or pounding, and fewer off-limit areas to reach by climbing. Although climbing, throwing, and pounding remain potentially destructive and always require supervision, children can be given greater leeway outdoors to test themselves against the world of objects.

A variety of outdoor environments is available for exercising new muscle power. Water can be splashed in a wading pool, and dirt can be pounded with the back of a small shovel. A toddler can tap on the garbage can, the backyard fence, or an old tree stump. Balls can be bounced in a driveway or thrown against the side of a garage. A small hill in the backyard makes a fine backboard for a large rubber ball. When your child

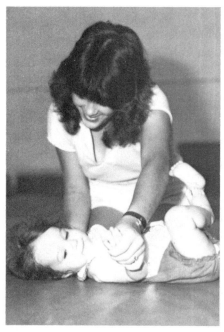

throws the ball up the hill, it comes back by itself. There are moderate, and reasonably safe, climbing opportunities: a sturdy picnic bench, a pile of sand, the steps of a toddler slide. Parks and other outdoor spaces can be explored. Simply walking around the block will bring out new opportunities for physical feats.

Gym environments, when they are available, are also excellent for a one-year-old's muscle power. Toddlers can climb on an apparatus designed for short legs and can try out all sorts of walking, balancing, sliding, and jumping skills. They can throw balls with gusto. They can push and pull. In some toddler gyms, even pounding opportunities are provided. The growing popularity of these gyms reflects our increased recognition that one-year-olds have the need and the right to practice all of their physical skills.

PLAY IDEAS

In this section we have looked at the ways young children explore and expand their muscle power. As with other aspects of exploration, you will seek to achieve a balance between setting limits and allowing your toddler free rein. In reaching this balance point, power struggles can take place, especially during the first flush of enthusiasm over a new physical skill. As you describe your child's physical feats, you also foster language skills by combining actions and words.

The play ideas we suggest describe ways to help children practice their newly acquired motor skills: pushing, pulling, and lifting; throwing and pounding; and working out.

Pushing, Pulling, and Lifting

Tetherball

Use a bath towel or plastic holders from soda cans to make a net. Put a large rubber ball in the net and suspend it from the ceiling or door frame. Your child will have fun batting the tetherball back and forth.

Push Toy

Sooner or later, one-year-olds seem to try pushing furniture around the house. Not only is much of it too heavy, but it is also not made to be pushed. A sofa bolster is an exception to the rule. It is light, rolls easily when pushed, and hurts nothing. Encourage your one-year-old, who is challenging the furniture, to lug and push a sofa bolster. If one is not available, try substituting a sleeping bag or a beach ball.

Pull Toy

The primary appeal of pull toys is their novelty. You can create a supply of new pull toys simply by attaching different objects to a rope. An empty lemon juice container or shampoo bottle makes a fine pull toy. You can also make a pull train out of cereal or shoe boxes, egg cartons, or gallon milk jugs.

Vehicle Roll

Of course, one of the favorite push toys of children is a toy car or truck. Small vehicles tend to be driven over pieces of furniture. A kitchen table provides a particularly fine play arena. The cars and trucks roll easily across the surface and form interesting configurations as they are positioned or parked on the table.

Riding Toys

Pushing and steering a large wheeled toy represents an exciting challenge for a one-year-old. Whether she sits on the toy and pushes with her feet or walks behind and pushes, you will see her mastering this challenge step by step. Given practice, she

will learn to reverse directions when she runs into a wall, negotiate tight turns and narrow doorways, and retrace a path or complete a circular route. These toys come in many forms, and one-year-olds seem to enjoy all of them.

Weight Lifting

The sense of power that drives one-year-olds to push and pull large objects also compels them to try lifting and carrying heavy loads. These weight-lifting experiments are most successful when an object looks heavier than it really is. Lifting an empty briefcase or hoisting a large inflatable toy gives an obvious boost to your one-year-old's feelings of pride and accomplishment.

Climbing

Soft Mountain

If you have a young toddler who wants to climb, put pillows or bean bag chairs in the corner of a room. This will give her a safe experience.

Look-Out

Many one-year-olds like to climb up on furniture and then stand on it. Parents typically discourage this behavior. An exception that makes sense is letting your child stand on furniture in order to look out the window. Even a young toddler can balance herself on a sofa and look out the living room window at passing motorists, school children, and neighborhood dogs. An older toddler is coordinated enough to stand on a plush armchair and look out other windows in the house. Being able to see what is going on in the outside world adds a new dimension to your child's daily routine and may occupy a considerable period of time.

Jumping Spot

Another reason for climbing on furniture is to be able to jump back down. Perhaps you and your child can find a place in the house for this climbing and jumping. One possibility is to remove a cushion from the couch. Your child can use this shallow pit as a jumping platform. Because the cushion has been removed, the couch is subject to less abuse. With a young toddler, you may want to build up the landing spot with a pillow; a fall of a few inches is tantalizing enough. As your child grows older, he will look for drop-offs of one to two feet.

Water Bed Climb

Children try to climb on beds as soon as they are able. Waterbeds seem to be even more popular with one-year-olds than traditional beds. They tend to be lower, which makes them easier to climb on, and they respond to the movements of the child. Regardless of the type of bed, parents worry that their

one-year-olds will fall and hurt themselves on the frame or the floor. Some parents manage this problem by closely watching their children and teaching them to play in the middle of the bed. Others establish a routine of playing with their child. Although some accidents still occur, most toddlers and their parents find that a bed, and especially a water bed, is an irresistible climbing toy.

Bridge Walk

Some one-year-olds like to climb on the couch and then walk back and forth, treating the couch like a bridge or a ledge. You can create this kind of climbing opportunity by placing the bottom pillows of the couch on the floor end-to-end. As your child becomes more adept, you may want to make the bridge walk more challenging by placing one of the bottom pillows on top of the other. Most of the time, one-year-olds are aware of their limitations and will explore a new bridge cautiously. If a new bridge intimidates your child, make the task easier by placing the balance beam next to a wall.

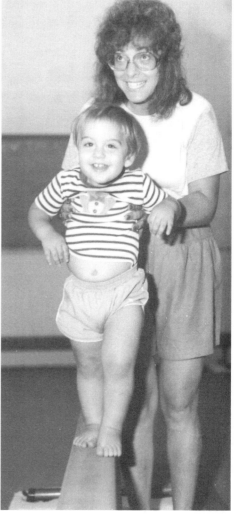

Throwing and Pounding

Bean Bag Toss

You can make a bean bag by filling a heavy-duty plastic sandwich bag with rice, macaroni, or oatmeal. Seal the bean bag with plastic tape. (Do not let your child put the bean bag near his mouth.) Create a target for bean bag throwing. A chair or wastebasket will work well. You can create an even more challenging target by cutting holes large enough for the bean bag to pass through in the side of a carton. Throwing at a safe target keeps indoor throwing within manageable limits.

Back Yard Toss

If your one-year-old continues to throw too many things indoors, you may want to work harder at transferring this behavior to an outdoor setting. Few activities have greater appeal

than throwing objects into water. Put a wading pool in a shady spot and let your child practice throwing whatever small objects are available in abundance: rocks, nuts, pine cones, crabapples. Some mess will result, but your child's penchant for throwing will not cause damage, and both of you will be happier. If there is snow on the ground, a snow pile is a perfect place for throwing.

Work Force

A toy workbench is good for letting one-year-olds hammer vigorously, but it means that the child's exploration must be restricted to one spot. Your child may have more fun with a miniature tool set. Whether made of plastic, hard rubber, or even metal, these tiny tools are not big enough to cause much damage. Still, one-year-olds see them as comparable to real tools and are satisfied pounding and poking all over the house. In fact, as older toddlers begin to pretend to fix things, they actually seem to prefer tools that cannot possibly have any effect. Perhaps it is easier to maintain the illusion that way.

Sand Pound

A one-year-old can use a flat tool, like a spatula or the back of a shovel, to firm and shape sand. Besides, it is just plain fun to pound on sand. When your toddler is in a hammering mood, let him beat on a sandpile for a while.

Exercising New Muscle Power at the Park or Gym

Your home is not always well suited to the outbursts of new muscle power from your one-year-old. The equipment at a park or gym, on the other hand, has been designed for just this purpose. Give your child regular opportunities to explore these muscle-building environments, and when you and your toddler are in conflict at home over a specific form of vigorous exploration, try to find an alternative outlet at the park or the gym.

Working Out

If you enjoy working out, let your toddler join the fun. Put a mat on the floor and let her exercise beside you. Use paper towel spindles as weights.

Reciting a chant makes exercising fun. When your toddler is on her back, help her bicycle with her legs as you recite:

> *Bicycle, bicycle, fast, fast, fast*
> *This is the way we go.*
> *Bicycle, bicycle, right to town*
> *And now we're going slow.*
> *Fast, slow, fast, slow, this is so much fun.*
> *And now we stop our bicycle*
> *Because our ride is done.*

If your toddler has learned to squat, hold on to her hands and play a squatting game. This is a good exercise for parents and toddlers alike.

> *Bend our knees, and down we go*
> *All the way to the floor.*
> *Up, up, up, we stand up tall,*
> *And now we squat some more.*

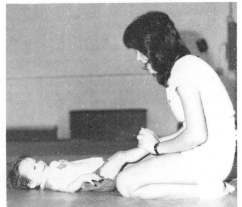

CHAPTER 4

The Timid or Fussy Explorer

The Scene: A public beach on Sunday

Father (carrying a picnic basket, several beach towels, an overstuffed teddy bear, and a diaper bag): "It was quite a ride, but it's worth it. This place is gorgeous and Courtney will love playing in the sand!"

Mother (putting Courtney down): "Feel the sand between your toes. Doesn't it feel good?"

Courtney (after standing in the sand for a second): "Upie, upie. Dadda upie. Go home."

Throughout the first chapters, we have emphasized the role of parents in setting limits and establishing rules. Children, however, are not always enthusiastic about independent exploration. Some children are disturbed by new sensations. Like Courtney, they are timid about new experiences such as loud noises, bright lights, or unusual textures. The sound of waves pounding on the shore or the flash of a camera may send them into a panic. Parents naturally want their children to conquer what seem to be illogical fears. We need to remember, however, that adult perceptions of "safe" and "dangerous" are not the same as those of a toddler. Just as you help your child avoid activities that look safe but really are dangerous, you will want to help him explore situations that may appear dangerous from a toddler's perspective but are really very safe.

The frightening nature of a strange stimulus can sometimes be blotted out by introducing more familiar sensations. Loud fireworks, for example, are less fear-provoking when par-

ents clap loudly and cheer after each explosion. This technique essentially involves distracting children, redirecting their attention. A one-year-old may stand uncertainly in a wading pool, apparently immobilized by the cold water. Then, when the parent directs the child's attention toward slapping the water and making splashes, the child forgets the unusual feel of the pool and starts exploring.

At other times, parents can help fearful one-year-olds with words, not so much by talking them out of their fear but by offering the right labels. Being able to label the fearful or disagreeable element in a situation gives young children a sense of power. The wading pool is "cold," the camera flash is "bright," ocean waves are "loud," sand is "scratchy." The particular words that parents use are not as important as the tone of confidence with which they are spoken. Seeing that a problem can be captured with words, one-year-olds try to imitate and feel more in control.

Probably the most effective technique of all is to desensitize fearful children. By exposing them to situations that are similar, but not as frightening, parents can help one-year-olds gradually learn to expand their range of exploration. The child who avoids sand at the beach can be exposed to a sandbox at home; the child who dislikes grass at the park can play on a blanket on the front lawn. A fear of bright light may be alleviated by giving your child a flashlight; a fear of loud noises may be lessened by giving him a big bell. There are no magic an-

swers, no series of precise steps to be followed in desensitizing a fearful one-year-old. You must simply try different ideas as you think of them, keeping in mind that it will take time for your child to overcome fears.

Older toddlers may show a different pattern of fearfulness. Suddenly and unpredictably, they are afraid of unusual creatures: clowns, automated characters, large animals. There is still a perceptual dimension to this fear in that the feared objects look and sound different but, beyond that, the children are worried about what these creatures might do. No longer so naive about the world, the children seem to imagine that the unusual creatures will hurt them. They are losing their innocence and the specter of "monsters" is clearly on the horizon.

Because toddlers sometimes are so funny when they first develop a baseless fear, opening their eyes like saucers or diving into their parent's lap, family members may be tempted to tease them with the awesome object. Karen screamed at the sight of a Halloween mask. Her older brother and sister, who knew that the mask was harmless, took turns putting on the mask to watch their sister's reactions. This kind of repeated experience can produce a long-lasting fear that may be difficult to modify.

It is better to help children get familiar with scary things in a gradual way. Pamela was petrified when she first encountered Mickey Mouse on a trip to Disney World. Back in the motel room, Pam's mother eased her fear by showing her Mickey Mouse's picture in a book and then buying her a miniature mouse. That afternoon Pam was given a chance to pet a larger Mickey Mouse in the toy store. By the end of the trip, Pamela bravely touched "real" Mickey Mouse's hand with the tip of her index finger.

In addition to gradual exposure, there are a variety of techniques to help your child overcome imaginary fears. You can hold him firmly in your arms as you approach the frightening object, or let him watch the object from a safe distance. You can associate a positive word like "pretty" with the scary thing, or tell your child to wave goodbye as soon as it appears. Knowing that Gretchen was afraid of beards, Gretchen's mother would say "There's a man with a beard over there. Let's wave goodbye." These techniques, without forcing one-year-olds to interact with frightening people, puppets, or animals, help children gain a sense of control.

In general, fearfulness is relatively uncommon at this stage. More common is fussiness, a condition hard to describe but easy enough for parents to recognize. Instead of getting into focused, independent exploration, the one-year-old is at loose ends, casting about for something to do. Often the child whines and hangs on a parent's leg. Earlier chapters have suggested activities for just such situations. Naturally each child will not enjoy all of these activities, but there will be some from each chapter that are appealing.

Some children are always on the lookout for objects with buttons to push. Others enjoy exploring substances with different textures: water, ice, mud, and different foods. Still others experiment with rearranging or changing things around. By recognizing and responding to your child's preferences, you can help focus his exploration, empowering him to design his own experiments and make his own discoveries.

PLAY IDEAS

One-year-olds differ from each other in the types of explorations they enjoy, the pace of their explorations, and the gusto with which they explore. In Play Ideas we describe materials and activities that encourage exploration and discovery.

Water Play

Of all the materials that toddlers explore, water seems to be the most interesting and versatile. Water play can soothe restlessness, dissipate whininess, or heighten excitement. Some situations, like playing in the bathtub, require parental supervision, but many forms of water play allow toddlers to play independently for long periods of time. The following pictures suggest the variety of activities that are possible.

- Water with pots and pans
- Pouring in the bathtub
- Pretend cooking in the bathtub
- Filling the wading pool
- Playing with a floating bridge in the wading pool
- Washing toys with soap bubbles

• Water painting
• Washing rocks in a bucket
• Washing a riding toy
• Playing with a hose

Pet Play

While some toddlers lack even appropriate fear of dogs and cats, other children cling to their parents when they hear the most distant bark. Getting timid explorers comfortable with pets cannot happen all at once. There are many ways, however, to help toddlers gain some level of confidence.

- Buy a toddler a non-frightening pet, like a goldfish, and let him participate in the feeding.
- Visit a small pet store where the animals are in cages. Talk about the animals you see.
- Visit a friend who has an old, gentle, and sleepy dog. Hold you toddler in your arms and let him pat its head.

Touching Techniques

If your toddler is concerned about getting dirt on his hands or touching something slimy or sticky, let him explore with a paint brush or long-handled spoon. Once he has become familiar with the things he is exploring, he will be less upset about getting it on his hands.

Companion Walk

When a toddler is tentative about new experiences, such as going to the beach or walking through snow, it helps to bring along a companion, like a doll or a teddy bear. Parents can let the teddy bear take the lead. "Touch the snow, Teddy. It's soft and cold." Then turning to their toddler, "I think Teddy likes the snow. Let's help him touch it again."

EVERYDAY LIVING

Introduction

~~~~~~

The Scene: The dining room in Grandmother's house.

Grandmother: "Now, Gina." (Picking up Gina, who is fifteen months old.) "How would you like to sit in this nice new highchair?"

Gina: "Mommy!"

Grandmother: "I guess she's not used to me yet. You better put her in the highchair."

Mother: "No, that's not the problem. She thinks she's too big for a highchair." (The crisis is averted by putting a telephone book on a kitchen chair.)

Later:

Grandmother (responding to Gina's whining): "What's the matter, honey? Would you like a glass of milk?"

Mother: "No, I think she's had it. I'll take her to the other room and nurse her."

Gina, like all one-year-olds, is ambivalent about growing up. At dinner time, she wanted to be big like everyone else, and she rejected the highchair emphatically. After dinner, she enjoyed the comfort of breast feeding and, in this respect, had no interest in being grown-up.

The ambivalence of a toddler puts parents in a double bind. On the one hand, they want their child to reach a new level of independence. On the other hand, they do not want to ignore their child's need for security and nurturing. As parents struggle to achieve an appropriate balance between independence and dependence, there are bound to be some strains in the parent-child relationship. Contributing to the problem is the fact that children do not usually progress in a straight line as they move toward independence. At twelve months, a child may go to sleep quite independently. Several months later, however, she might start waking in the middle of the night and insisting on parental reassurance. A toddler who has been feeding herself may revert to whining and wanting to be fed. These apparent regressions should be expected and often signal a spurt in one or more developmental domains. They also tend to be short lived. When a child regresses in one or more domains, a good rule of thumb is to go back to the strategies that were successful when your baby was younger.

CHAPTER 5

Everyday Routines

The Scene: In the kitchen.

Father (to Mother): "Jean, why don't you go and get dressed? I'll give Timmy his supper."

Timothy: "Ghetti-oos."

Father: "Here's your spaghetti. Do you want juice?"

Timothy: "Ye-oos."

Father: "Okay, here's your glass of apple juice."

Timothy (throwing the glass on the floor): "No oos. No!"

Father: "Timothy, make up your mind. You want milk?"

Timothy (shouting): "Want oos."

Mother (hearing the shouting, returns to the kitchen): "Timothy likes his juice in the Big Bird cup."

This chapter describes the daily routines of eating, sleeping, dressing, and cleaning up. When your toddler was an infant, daily routines provided special opportunities for you to communicate with your child. Diapering, dressing, and bathing were opportunities to play, and putting your infant to sleep was a special opportunity to cuddle. Daily routines with toddlers require a different approach. While there are still opportunities for interactive play and cuddling, the routines of daily living can also turn into hassles.

In this chapter, we look at routines from a developmental point of view. What is your baby doing or attempting to master as he practices or resists a routine? What does your baby's reaction to routines tell you about his temperament? How do child-

rearing beliefs and style guide the management of care-giving routines? How do individual differences in temperament affect a toddler's willingness to accept routines?

Conflicts inevitably arise as children develop new capacities to take an active part in daily routines. These conflicts occur when parents expect too much, or when children backslide in their independence. They may also occur when parents do not allow their child to change things for himself, or when a child's demand to do everything himself assumes unreasonable proportions. Unquestionably, some conflicts generate negative feelings on the part of both parents and toddlers. At the same time, daily living with a toddler produces intense positive emotions.

Taking care of a toddler is a time-consuming and demanding job. In this chapter, we focus on prominent care-giving routines, recognizing, of course, that care giving is never completely routine. Challenges vary from day to day, from situation to situation, and certainly from family to family. But despite these variations, all families with one-year-olds share some of the same concerns and face the same types of challenges. The purpose of this chapter is to look more closely at the variety of ways families meet these challenges.

In any family with a toddler, it is not unusual to hassle over eating, sleeping, dressing, or some other daily routine. We overheard, for example, a fairly typical conversation between two mothers.

Michael's mother: "You're lucky Veronica eats so well. My Michael is such a picky eater, he drives me crazy."
Veronica's mother: "Who cares about eating? It's sleeping we're having a problem with. Your Michael at least sleeps through the night."

Immersed in a crisis over a particular routine, you can easily lose perspective and forget how much progress your child is making. The toddler period is a time of transition, when children grow from helpless infants to surprisingly self-sufficient two-year-olds. Sleeping, eating, and other routines gradually change as children take on more responsibility for self management. Naturally, progress is uneven, and all children regress at times. But if you keep in mind this larger pattern of development, you are less likely to exaggerate the significance of specific problems.

SLEEPING

Going to sleep seems to be the most habit forming of all routines. By the time children are one year old they already have a well-established routine that helps them relax and fall asleep. For some children, this routine is short and simple—a bath, a bottle of water or milk, a goodnight kiss, and then into their

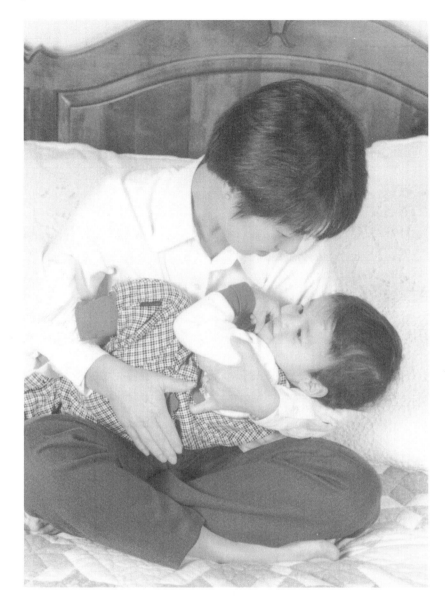

crib. In other families, a different pattern is present. Ever since the children were infants, going to sleep has been a time of emotional intimacy between parents and children. The children have been rocked or nursed for an extended period before being placed in the crib. Often, parents have developed the

habit of singing to their child, watching television together, or talking quietly with him.

In families where going to sleep is treated matter-of-factly, relatively few sleep problems are reported. The children may go through brief stages of resisting bedtime, but for the most part they go to sleep easily once they are in bed. In families where bedtime is associated with intimate interaction, there is a greater likelihood of procrastination. Both parents and children think of bed time as a special time to be together and are not in a hurry to give up this special time.

Regardless of their philosophy and their style, parents discover some techniques that help one-year-olds accept bedtime. A common technique is to include a stuffed animal in the bedtime routine. In the simplest form of the ritual, parents just give the child a stuffed animal when they say goodnight. Often the routine becomes more elaborate. In Kenneth's family, for instance, Stuffy Bear participates in the entire bedtime preparation. First Stuffy Bear puts on his pajamas, then he gets his teeth brushed, and finally, if he has been a very good bear, he can have a little sip of water.

A second technique many parents use is reading a bedtime story. The children get ready for bed, select a book, and then sit beside their parent while the story is read. Obviously, the routine becomes elaborated as parents and children share a greater number of stories. If the books are left with the child after the parents leave the room, the children often continue to read by themselves. One-year-olds, like their parents, enjoy reading in bed.

Of course, one-year-olds find bedtime most acceptable when there is physical contact with parents. Rocking, nursing, or holding are effective ways to induce relaxation. But a problem may arise with these comfort strategies when parents try to transfer their children to the crib. The children have grown so accustomed to physical contact that they wake up as soon as the contact is broken. If this kind of bedtime routine is selected, it is a good idea to transfer your toddler before he is fully asleep. Over time he will learn to enjoy falling asleep on his own.

Some parents avoid bedtime problems by letting their babies sleep in their bed. This works well so long as both parents are comfortable with it. In many cultures putting young children to sleep in the family bed is standard practice.

Changing to a Big Bed

Sometimes parents, with the best of intentions, decide it is time for their toddler to move from a crib to a regular bed. If the child associates this change with being grown-up, the crib may be abandoned without tears. If, however, the child resists the new bed, parents suddenly find themselves in the midst of a sleep-time problem. In this situation parents are best off moving slowly. For a while both the crib and the bed can be left in the room. The child can be encouraged to nap in the bed, while continuing to sleep in the crib at night. When the toddler seems ready to move into the bed at night, the crib blanket and other accessories can be taken along.

Exchanging a crib for a bed is a big change for toddlers and should be planned when other big changes are not taking place. Julia's parents told us about a mistake they made when they moved to a new house. Julia had been involved in setting up her room in the new house and seemed excited about everything: her closet with shelves, the Disney World curtains, and her own big bed. Moving day went fine until bedtime. As her father put her down in the bed, Julia started sobbing, "No bed, no night-night, go home." Her parents realized immediately that adjusting to a new house and a new bed at the same time was more than Julia could handle.

Middle-of-the-Night Problems

Nighttime awakening is a very frequent problem with toddlers. Many children cry out in apparent fright or anger as they sleep. Some parents decide to go to the crib and reassure their child. These parents reason that responding to the crying helps a child feel more secure and sustains the bond of trust. Picking up the child, or simply staying in the bedroom for a few minutes, is usually sufficient. When it is not sufficient, these parents are likely to let their toddler sleep with them. This practice usually works as long as the parents are willing to keep it up.

A second approach that parents use is to let their child cry when he awakens at night. Their hope is that their child will go back to sleep by himself. These parents reason that responding too quickly will encourage nighttime waking. As evidence, they point to the fact that, after a few days or weeks of sporadic crying, nighttime waking diminishes. Having found that company is not forthcoming, their child learns to get back to sleep on his own.

As with other routine problems, there is no one, correct way to handle middle-of-the-night problems. Children at this age are easily reassured if responded to quickly but, at the same time, responding to every call can establish a habit. The appropriate decision for parents depends on the priorities they have already set. If intimacy at bedtime is a high priority, it makes sense for them to get up and answer the child's call or let the child sleep in their bed. If a straightforward sleep routine is their preference, it makes sense to make sure their child is all right and then let him cry it out for a few minutes. Whatever your style when putting a one-year-old to bed in the first place, it seems best to continue that approach in the middle of the night.

There are times, however, when the approach that parents prefer does not work, and nighttime awakening increases steadily. This situation seems to occur most often with breast-fed children, who may get up every hour or two for a few moments of nursing. Marietta's parents told us that when Marietta began waking up several times a night, both mother and father tried everything in the book to dissuade her from nursing: offering her a cup of warm milk, turning on a radio in her room, buying her a new stuffed animal to sleep with, and putting a night-light in her room. Nothing helped. Marietta just screamed until she was nursed. Finally, their pediatrician suggested that they close the door and let her cry. The first three nights were terrible, but by the fourth night Marietta slept through the night without a whimper.

Although the decision to let a child cry it out is difficult to make, it is not necessarily wrong. If a toddler's sleeping habits are out of hand, and the family is exhausted, it is important for parents to assert more control. At the same time, remember that bedtime problems and sleeping routines are never completely controllable. Parents may prefer a straightforward routine, while their child pushes for an extended period of interaction before going to sleep. Parents may introduce the idea of reading a bedtime story, only to find that their child is not interested. Despite parents' ability to guide sleeping routines, the eventual outcome in any particular situation will be a collaborative effort between parent and child.

EATING

In the first year, babies are hungry at fairly predictable times and show little evidence of strong likes and dislikes. Parents are in charge of their baby's limited diet, and creating good eating habits is not an issue. During the second year, all this changes. Children are not as hungry, and their appetites fluctuate erratically. They are likely to become increasingly sensitive to taste and texture, and are increasingly selective about the food they will eat. Children who are slow to master the art of chewing may reject meat and other solid foods. Children who are sensitive to texture may dislike foods like cottage cheese or custard, which are neither liquid nor solid.

Parents tend to respond to these changes with a new concern over nutrition. They want to be sure that their children eat a well-balanced diet, and they hope that they will sample a variety of foods. Additional clashes may occur over junk food. Although parents can keep junk food away from their toddlers without too much difficulty, the children are beginning to be aware of these food treats. Naturally, parents, in their desire to instill good eating habits, do not want their children "hooked" on foods heavy in salt or sugar.

Parents handle eating conflicts in different ways. Miranda's mother describes her daughter, at eighteen months, as a "finicky eater." Frequently Miranda looks suspiciously at the food on her highchair tray and refuses to try even one bite. Both her parents then introduce some kind of game to get her to eat. The meal may begin with, "One bite for Mommy and one bite for Miranda," or Dad's spoon may become a "chug-a-lug-choo-choo" that feeds Miranda while entertaining her.

Rachel, at eighteen months, goes through spells of eating with enthusiasm and spells of eating very little. Her parents, however, avoid urging her to eat when she is not hungry. If Rachel begins to play with her food or throw it on the floor, her mother takes her out of the high chair. "She'll eat if she's hungry," her mother insists, "and I'm not going to make a big deal over food."

When comparing these two families, it is evident that Rachel's parents are more relaxed about eating routines. They have decided that prompting Rachel to eat when she's not hungry makes little sense. Instead, they concentrate on giving her a wide selection of nutritious foods, and then leaving the choice about eating in Rachel's hands. In short, Rachel's parents are confident that, eventually, Rachel will self-select an adequate diet.

For parents like Miranda's, who find it difficult to be this relaxed about the eating habits of their one-year-old, there are other techniques that may smooth over potential conflicts. Food can be cut into very small bites or thin slices. Raw vegetables, fruits, and pieces of meat are more palatable in this form because the texture and taste are diluted. Parents can suggest a condiment, such as catsup or mayonnaise, for a piece of meat that is ignored by a one-year-old. Parents can also provide meat substitutes that require little preparation, such as eggs, cheese,

or yogurt. Some parents keep a supply of fishsticks or leftover chicken on hand to offer their child when the family eats something more difficult to chew. A technique that works especially well is to place some of the toddler's food on the parent's plate and have the parent eat it with exaggerated relish.

There is an almost endless variety of ways to make food more appealing, but in every case parents run the risk of over emphasizing the importance of eating. Nowhere is this risk more evident than when parents bribe their children to eat. Offering a treat for eating a nutritional food may work in the short run. Soon, however, the children learn to eat the smallest possible amount in order to receive the reward. In general, we advise parents to be patient when children reject their food. There will be other meals, and the old adage of waiting to try another day is a good philosophy.

Eating routines are also social occasions. During the second year, many parents grow concerned about *how* a child is eating as well as *what* the child is eating. This is especially true if the toddler is eating dinner with the family. Parents find themselves reminding their children about lapses in table manners. "You don't eat vanilla pudding with your fingers. You don't put your carrot in the milk jug. You don't lick the dish with your tongue."

Although it may not always be evident, your one-year-old is making a start toward good table manners. He is learning to use a spoon and fork, and he enjoys using a napkin to clean up messes he has made. If he hears "please" and "thank you" at the table, he may surprise you by using these words. More importantly, your toddler is learning that eating routines are a

time when the family comes together to share their food and their feelings. Wanting to be a part of this sharing, he may try to join a conversation by yelling louder than anyone else, or try to attract your attention by performing various antics. With patience and a sense of humor, though, this exuberance can be kept in bounds and meals with your toddler can be a pleasant time for interaction.

Weaning is another area of potential conflict in some families. At some time during the second year, mothers may choose to wean their baby. They would like to return to work, or the baby has sharp teeth, or perhaps they feel that breast feeding or drinking from a bottle is fine for babies, but too babyish for toddlers. In other families the situation is reversed. A mother believes that her toddler is too young to wean, and the toddler insists on a cup.

Weaning breast-fed children is usually more difficult than weaning bottle-fed babies. Experienced mothers tell us that the best way to be successful with weaning is to cut down gradually, stretching out the time between feedings. Abrupt weaning is hard on both mother and child. A question that nursing mothers often ask is whether to bypass the bottle and go directly to the cup. Here, the rationale for weaning comes into play. If the mother wants her toddler to be more grown-up, it is logical to introduce a glass or cup. If the mother gives up nursing for practical reasons, switching to a bottle may be easier. In either case, the child's own preference needs to be taken into account. Where a one-year-old shows a definite preference, weaning is a lot smoother if this choice is respected.

Obviously, when a toddler and parent have different ideas about weaning there has to be a compromise. A mother can entice her toddler into continuing to nurse by reserving nursing for times when her baby is sleepy. On the other hand, she can help her toddler give up the bottle or breast by letting him have a small drink from a favorite cup before settling down to nurse.

Whether the decision to wean is initiated by a mother or her toddler, it is less traumatic if it is a gradual process. If a mother makes the decision to wean her toddler, it is important to seek out ways to make a cup more attractive than nursing or a bottle. Ideas suggested by parents include buying a special cup, inviting over a toddler who drinks from a cup, watering down a bottle, or pretending the teddy bear is drinking from a cup.

Steven's mother tried a different approach that turned out to be quite successful. She pretended to drink from a baby bottle while Steven was watching. Steven laughed at this silly scene and from then on refused to drink out of a bottle.

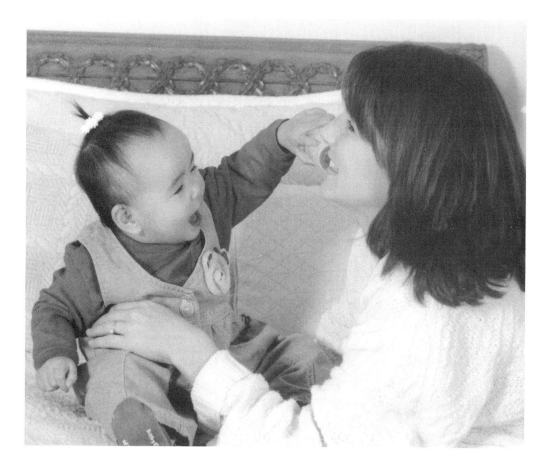

DRESSING

For parents, dressing routines represent the process of making a one-year-old presentable. This process includes selecting and putting on appropriate clothes, combing and brushing hair, and washing hands and face.

For many toddlers, looking nice is not important. Getting dressed is a bother, and having one's hair brushed or one's face washed is even more senseless. With many children, their attitudes about dressing routines change as they approach the age of two. Children are likely to adopt a favorite outfit, and they recognize the compliment in words like "pretty" or "cute." They dimly understand that coats and sweaters really are useful in cold weather. It is apparent that a dry diaper feels better than a wet one. Of course, these insights are easy to forget. In the midst of an interesting activity, children are likely to ignore their wet diapers, abandon their coats, and play just as happily without their clothes as with them.

Toddlers tend to be more resistant about dressing when the family is in a hurry. They become experts at squirming as

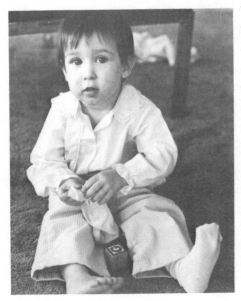

their diapers are changed, curling their toes in order to avoid shoes, dodging out of the way when it is time to brush hair, or turning their head from side to side when a parent approaches with a wash cloth. Parents usually can catch their child, but holding him still and putting his clothes on is another matter. In Timothy's family, when neither watching television nor holding the keys to the car reduced the squirming and twisting, Timothy's father got the idea of placing Timothy in front of a mirror. The idea worked. Timothy got interested in watching the transformation that took place as he was dressed. He even tolerated having his hair brushed. For Pamela, getting dressed turned into a game of making choices. Her mother would ask, "Would you like your Dolphins shirt or your Robin Hood shirt?" Brenan's grandmother took advantage of his burgeoning sense of humor when it was her turn to do the dressing. "Now, let's see," she began, "I'll put your nose in your sock. Oh, yes, and your shoe goes on your ear." "No, my foot," Brenan laughed, as he helped slide his foot in the shoe.

Perhaps the most effective technique for keeping one-year-olds still while you dress them is to sing a dressing song. "This is the way we put on your sock," (sung to the tune of "Here We Go Around the Mulberry Bush") is a standard favorite. As your child's ears strain to understand this novel form of communication, the rest of his body relaxes. The dressing routine, instead of being a tiresome interruption, becomes a special occasion.

Singing while dressing a one-year-old requires an extra measure of energy, but in the end it is far less of a drain than nagging the child to stay still. Gradually, as toddlers take a greater interest in their personal appearance, they participate more actively in dressing routines. They position their arms and legs to receive the clothes that parents are putting on. They may even try to put on certain items of clothing by themselves, such as shoes, hats, or coats.

When all is said and done, however, most one-year-olds remain basically disinterested in dressing routines. Their enthusiasm lies in undressing. It is so much easier to take shoes off than to get them back on, to strip off a coat than to put it on. Parents can foster dressing skills in a one-year-old by supporting this interest in undressing. Undressing routines can be established just as well as dressing ones. Bath time, for example, is a prime opportunity for children to take off their clothes and enjoy a brief period of naked cavorting.

BATH TIME

Most toddlers love taking a bath and will stay in the tub for as long as parents will keep an eye on them. Once in a while, however, a one-year-old becomes terrified of the bathtub. Parents who face this problem need not feel that their child is peculiar. The line between excitement and terror is a thin one. Any exciting activity can quickly become frightening, whether it is a one-year-old playing in water, a teenager riding a roller coaster, or an adult speaking in public. Some experience with water has pushed these children over the line, and it takes a long time for them to overcome their fear. A number of alternatives can be tried to entice a fearful child into the bathtub, but the best antidote is arranging for the child to watch other young children taking a bath. Gradually the fearful child can be encouraged to join these peers (cousins are even better) in the bathtub.

The potential scariness of water is quite apparent in the reaction of most toddlers to hair washing. Soap in their eyes on one or two occasions is enough to make hair washing a major ordeal. Some parents have overcome hair washing fears by using a novel container. One mother used a watering can to rinse her child's hair; another parent used a tea kettle. Pretending to wash a doll's hair may also help with the problem. A special song may be reserved for rinsing out the soap, such as "I'm Gonna Wash That Soap (Man) Right Out of My Hair." Once children become fearful, however, parents cannot expect any technique to be immediately successful. As with other fears, time will be needed to convert anxiety back into excitement, and parents need to be willing to experiment with a variety of techniques.

TOILET LEARNING

Since the advent of disposable diapers, many parents do not even consider toilet training until children are almost two, and even then they approach it with a casual attitude. In general, older toddlers are interested in imitating the behavior of other people, which means that they may enjoy imitating parents and siblings by sitting on the toilet. If a child sits there long enough, this imitation will produce results.

The imitative style of a toddler has other possibilities as well. Gretta, who had little interest in sitting on the potty seat, was interested in toilet training her dolls. Each doll was given a turn on the potty while Gretta made "sss" noises. Although Gretta was emphatic about not sitting on the potty herself, she obviously enjoyed this doll play as her mother explained, "One day she'll be ready and she'll let us know. At least for now, she feels comfortable in the bathroom."

PLAY IDEAS

As you read the sections in this chapter on sleeping, eating, bathing, dressing, and toilet training, you will select ideas that are both pertinent to the problems you are experiencing and compatible with your child-rearing beliefs. The daily routine in your family, as in every family, is a reflection of your style and your philosophy as a parent. Unquestionably, these routines provide challenges, but they also provide opportunities for parents and their toddlers to share moments of intimacy.

Our goal in this chapter has been to demonstrate that there are multiple approaches to almost any problem. Although every parent has favorite techniques for managing young children, caretaking problems are minimized when parents remain open to new ideas. At the same time, when parents are struggling to solve a problem they need to stick with a chosen technique long enough to give it a chance. Flexibility should be balanced with persistence. The secret to this balance is thoughtful communication between care givers, between mother and father, between mother and grandmother, between friends. Collectively, our care-giving expertise greatly exceeds what any of us can generate independently.

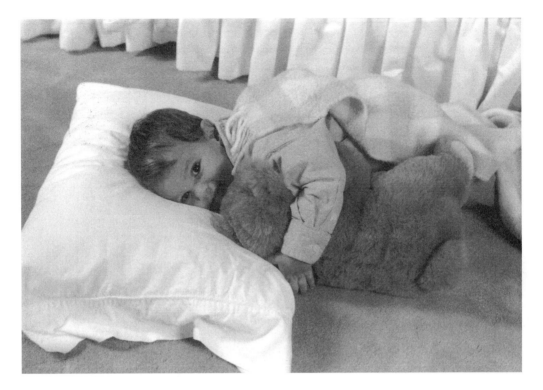

Bedtime Strategies

Bear Hug

If your toddler has moved into a regular bed, he may have a tendency to wander at night and end up sleeping in your bed. An extra-large stuffed animal, although not as reassuring as a parent, can eventually become a satisfactory substitute.

Goodnight Wave

Waving goodbye helps ease the pain of separation. You can give your child a way to say goodbye more intimately by showing him how to blow a kiss. This technique is especially helpful at bedtime. Your toddler gets one last intimate goodbye as you leave the bedroom.

Goodnight Moon

Heading toward the bed when it is bedtime can be a hassle. Try reenacting the theme of the popular book, *Goodnight Moon*. Help your toddler say goodnight to objects as you walk to the bedroom. Pick some favorites, some surprises, some objects outside the window: "Goodnight TV, goodnight tape, goodnight dandelions."

Night Play

Some toddlers naturally develop a habit of playing in their bed before and after sleep. Try putting different toys and books in your child's bed after he is asleep. Then watch to see if they are played with the next morning. As you discover what appeals to your child, introduce the materials at bedtime and allow your child time to play in bed before falling asleep.

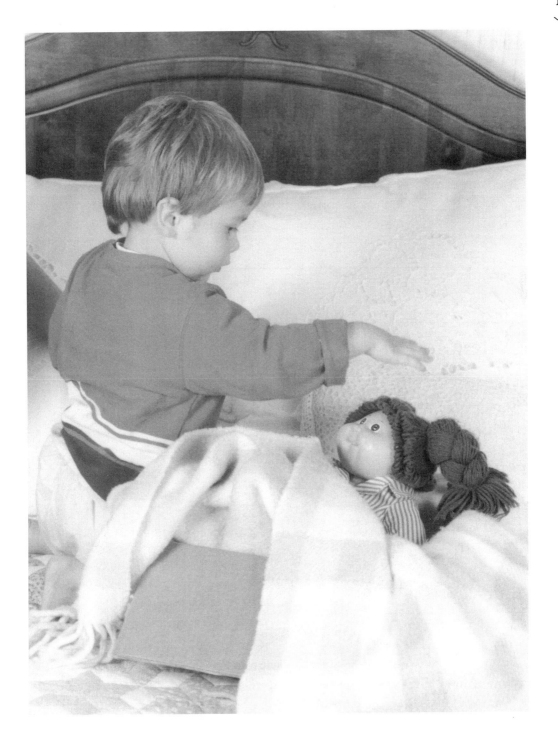

Mealtime Strategies

Encourage your toddler to feed himself, whether this means using a spoon and fork or only fingers. This will foster positive attitudes about eating.

One Bite For Mommy

As toddlers become more independent, they like to reverse the usual roles and feed their parents. This is one of many ways that parents and young children can share food. Sharing food does not mean that your toddler will eat more food, but it certainly reduces tension that can be built up at the dinner table.

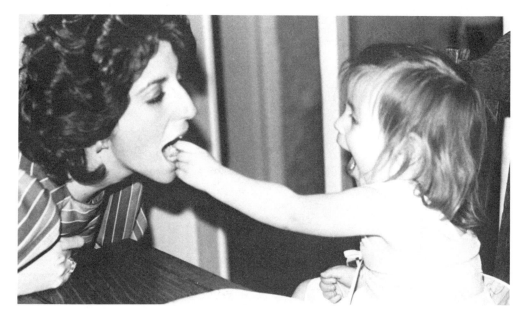

Taster

Before asking your toddler to try a new food, introduce it to a willing dinner guest or a favorite stuffed animal. Naturally the guest will be pleasantly surprised by this new food and heartily recommend it to the child.

Dressing Strategies

Mirror Play

Placing your toddler in front of a mirror may help him overlook the inconvenience of having his hair brushed. In fact, he may even begin to see a point to this custom.

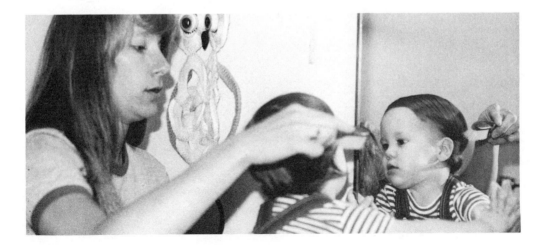

Clothes Selection

Your toddler may be hard to catch when it is time to change clothes. Perhaps he is expressing his independence by refusing to get dressed. You can help him associate independence with dressing by giving him a limited choice of clothing. Having committed himself to one shirt over another, it seems logical to put the shirt on.

Routine Sharing

Any daily routine is more appealing for your toddler if it is a social occasion. A one-year-old will enjoy sharing a moment of tooth-brushing with an older sibling.

Doll Dress

Dressing, like eating, can be played out with dolls and stuffed animals. Although toddlers are not usually able to dress a doll, they certainly can undress it.

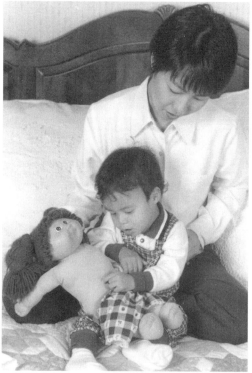

Stripping the clothes off a favorite stuffed animal is a good prelude to bedtime. First Teddy gets ready for bed, then Teddy's friend gets ready for bed.

Washcloth Puppet

Having his face washed can seem very intrusive to a toddler. If your toddler screams when you approach him with a washcloth, transform it into a hand puppet. "Hello, my name is Wendy the Washrag, what's your name?" Soon, your child may be willing to rub noses with this talking washcloth.

Goodbye Toes

If your toddler resists socks or shoes, talk to her toes: "Bye bye, toes, see you later."

Hat Show

One-year-olds are only beginning to learn how to dress themselves. You can help by encouraging your child to practice any dressing skill that spontaneously arises, whether it is trying on hats, putting one arm in the sleeve of a coat, or struggling to fit a foot into a shoe.

Toilet Strategies

House Breaking

If your toddler is not so sure he wants to sit on the toilet, show him how to put a doll or play animal on it. Reenacting the routine with dolls or play animals will help your child learn what is expected and make toilet learning more fun.

Toilet Toys

Once your child has agreed to sit on the toilet, find something interesting for him to do while he sits there. Kevin, at eighteen months, liked to spread skin cream on his legs as he sat on the potty. Alicia liked holding a wad of toilet tissue. Your child may enjoy holding a favorite toy or looking at a book.

Preschool Teacher

One of the best ways to introduce toilet learning is to encourage your child to go into the bathroom with someone else and watch what goes on. Toddlers especially like to accompany friends or siblings who are a year or two older than themselves. You will be surprised what good teachers preschool children can be.

Whatever technique you used, don't set your sights on getting your child trained. Very few one- to two-year-olds are ready for toilet learning. A realistic goal for parents is to ready their child for toilet learning by capitalizing on the child's desire to imitate, and by making a "toidy" seat safe and interesting.

CHAPTER 6

Helping Mom and Dad

The Scene: An outdoor barbecue.
Aunt: "Oh, isn't that adorable. Shannon is helping clean up. She's throwing the
*   paper napkins into the trash."*
Shannon: "De-dee-de-dee, mornin."
Mother: "She came to help. She's trying to sing, 'This is the way we wash our clothes,
*   early in the morning.' That's what we sing when we do the housework together."*
Aunt: "She's some little girl."
Shannon, having gathered up the last of the used napkins, makes a dive for the
*   package of clean ones.*
Mother: "No-no-no! Those napkins are clean. You do get carried away. Let's put
*   them back in the picnic basket. That's a big girl."*

Although your one-year-old's efforts to be helpful can some
times be worse than no help at all, it is fun to watch the
performance and natural to praise her effort. In the barbecue
scene, Shannon's napkin gathering was reinforced by both
Mother and Aunt, and even her attempt to toss out the new
napkins was treated with good humor. Shannon made up in enthusiasm whatever she lacked in job skills.

Toddlers are interested in any of the important jobs that
adults do. They want to turn on the stereo, drive the car, cut
with a knife, write with a pen, push the lawn mower, and operate the vacuum cleaner. These aspirations, while understandable, are hardly realistic. Having a young child underfoot when
you are trying to clean the house, mow the lawn, or cook the
dinner is anything but easy. In fact, the more insistent your

child is about helping, the more difficult it becomes to accomplish these routine chores.

In this chapter, we will discuss this dilemma by looking at three kinds of housework: doing the laundry, cooking, and cleaning up. Although these three chores encompass only a portion of the household work that parents and toddlers may share, they illustrate how different jobs lend themselves to different degrees of toddler participation. Doing the laundry includes several safe and simple tasks that toddlers can tackle. By contrast, cooking represents a much more dangerous activity in which participation usually is indirect or imaginary. Cleaning up, the third category, is less dangerous than cooking, but usually requires more supervision than typical laundry jobs.

DOING THE LAUNDRY

As we visited different families with toddlers, we found that many families had found ways to structure laundry chores so that a one-year-old could help. In nearly every family, children were encouraged to put dirty clothes in the hamper, although the consequences were not always what was expected. At Toni's house, for example, Toni's older sister, Gina, came into the living room complaining about having no socks. "Look in the dirty clothes hamper," Toni's mother suggested. Gina went compliantly back into the bedroom. According to Toni's mother, "Toni loves to help with the laundry, so we always

let her put the dirty clothes in the hamper. Sometimes she gets carried away and doesn't wait for the clothes to get dirty." A few minutes later Gina came out with her socks on, confirming her mother's hypothesis.

Sorting the laundry is another activity in which toddlers typically participate. Terry helped sort the dirty laundry into white and colored piles and then enthusiastically threw one pile into the washing machine. Andrea was able to separate the clothes from the dryer into Mom's pile, Dad's pile, and Andrea's pile.

Parents often encounter teasing behavior while sorting the laundry. The children will unfold the laundry as soon as their parents finish folding it. Or they pull clean clothing out of the drawer as soon as parents put it in. Obviously, children see no need to draw a sharp line between work and play. In their eyes, sorting and folding laundry is a form of play, and teasing is quite appropriate. Parents report that this kind of situation is made more manageable if the task is organized as a two-step operation. The parents will hand one small, folded item at a time to the child, who then places each item in the drawer. Describing the teamwork helps to keep the rhythm going. "One shirt coming up. One shirt in the drawer. Another shirt coming up!"

Of course, the most exciting part of doing the laundry is operating the washer and dryer. Under supervision, children can play the role of assistant operator. They can dump a cup of laundry powder in the washing machine and watch from a safe distance as the tub fills and begins to agitate. They can lend a hand when it comes time to haul the wet clothes out of the washing machine and transfer them to the dryer. They enjoy pushing the "on" button for the dryer and, when the job is done, they like to lean inside the warm, dark hole and fish out the dry clothes. Like many other laundry jobs, operating the washer and dryer involves a lot of emptying and filling. One-year-olds can participate easily because the work is a simple extension of a favorite theme in their spontaneous play.

COOKING

The kitchen is unquestionably the most dangerous spot in the house, and many parents feel that toddlers do not belong in it when food is being cooked. Toddlers, of course, hold quite a different view. In their opinion, the kitchen is a place where

interesting things happen, and when Mom or Dad is in the kitchen, that's just where they want to be.

Michael's mother told us that she has a firm rule about Michael staying out of the kitchen when dinner is being prepared. "Fortunately both my husband and I cook, and while one of us does the cooking, the other stays with Michael." Most

of the parents we visited, however, do not try to exclude their toddlers from the kitchen. Instead, they concentrate on finding techniques that will keep a young child busy in a safe way. With younger toddlers, the parents provide some floor level distractions while they work. A favorite distracter is a collection of colorful magnetic strips that stick to the refrigerator. (Magnetic letters or any type of magnet that could come out of its setting presents a swallowing hazard.) These magnetic strips are put away when parents are not cooking, so they become special toys associated with cooking time. Equally successful is a drawer or cupboard that contains kitchen items such as pots, pans, spoons, and measuring cups. A few families also keep a collection of appealing toys on a low kitchen shelf.

When parents are casual enough in the kitchen to intersperse their cooking with an occasional moment of play, one-year-olds may stay in this distractible stage for a long time. Your child may develop game routines for the kitchen and will be satisfied with this degree of involvement. For example, she may develop a game of hiding under the table until a parent finds her, or maneuvering a push toy around and around the table. Playing with pots and pans may evolve into pretend cooking, or she may pretend to feed a doll.

Eventually, however, toddlers grow taller and smarter. They notice that dramatic events are taking place on the countertop and stove burners, and they want to see what is going on. Sometimes parents let their children sit on the counter and watch. A better solution is a high chair or a Sassy Seat®. (If the Sassy Seat doesn't fit under the kitchen counter, try pulling out a drawer.) The most versatile watching posture is standing on a sturdy kitchen chair with arms. Assuming that the child is mature enough to stand steadily and that a parent assists the maneuvers, the chair can be moved from one vantage point to another.

Watching leads, in time, to wanting to share in the fun, and parents are faced with a one-year-old who expects to help cook. Occasionally children can help with the preparation phase of cooking. A child might join in stirring a cake mix, husking corn, or tearing lettuce for a salad. Parents can also satisfy their toddler's desire to be a part of the action by offering an activity that has the appearance, but not the substance, of kitchen work. A small quantity of flour and water in a bowl,

for example, makes a good mixing job. A wet sponge, a pan, and a dish towel make a toddler feel like part of the work force.

As Julia's mother demonstrated to us, the sink provides an excellent spot for redirecting the energies of older toddlers who want to help in the kitchen.

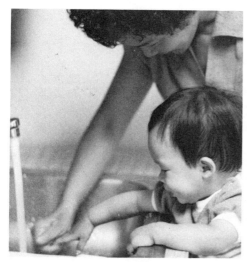

"First, I take off her clothes," Julia's mother began. "Then I fill the sink half full of water, turn the faucets off from underneath and let her play. By giving her a set of measuring cups and some serving spoons, I can get a whole meal prepared while she plays with the water. Of course, I never leave her alone when she is playing in the sink. My spouse and I share the cooking, and one of us watches Julia while the other prepares dinner." Other parents described similar discoveries. Liquid soap, when added to the water, created mounds of bubbles that could be ladled into plastic cups. Turning the water on just a little and letting a toddler play with the drain plug can prove engrossing.

The success of water play at the sink illustrates an important principle. One-year-olds are looking for an activity that is intrinsically interesting to them. They want to feel they are involved in kitchen work, but they are not really concerned about the work getting done. Beneath their imitative veneer, the children are most interested in exploratory play. By giving them a chance to explore either by watching or by manipulating a variety of interesting materials, parents can find a way to accommodate one-year-old helpers in the kitchen.

CLEANING HOUSE

When it comes to housecleaning, parents usually are in favor of having one-year-olds help to some degree, especially to begin the habit of picking up their toys. One-year-olds, however, seem to be less enthusiastic about this job than about other jobs they see parents doing. For one thing, there is no impressive technology associated with picking up: no buttons to push, no machines to operate. For another thing, children are often told to pick up their toys, which is quite different from volunteering to participate in an adult job.

Typically children in a school setting are asked to pick up right before a popular activity and, in this way, picking up becomes a rewarding task. Parents can do the same thing, scheduling a pleasant activity such as reading a story, eating, or going outside, right after picking up. Teachers also use music to signal cleaning up and to set an upbeat mood. A simple song, with made-up verses like, "Clean-up time, clean-up time, now it's time for clean-up time," works wonders with one-year-old children.

Extra incentives are not always needed for cleaning jobs. Your one-year-old may enjoy scrunching up papers and throwing things in the trash. Even better for some toddlers is the very grown-up task of carrying a trash bag to the garbage can. Toddlers can learn to pick up dirty napkins and plastic glasses and take them to the sink, or take placemats off the table and put them in the drawer. They can pick up the newspaper and bring it inside, or transfer spoons into and out of the dishwasher. Any of these adult forms of picking up appeal to a one-year-old's sense of self-importance.

Cleaning jobs that involve mechanical picking up are especially popular. Although some one-year-olds are frightened by a vacuum cleaner, many toddlers think the vacuum cleaner is the most exciting toy in the house. Children try to turn it on and push it. They sit or stand on it and take a ride. They squat in front of it and dare their parents to chase them. Unless the child chooses to hold the vacuum cleaner with you, her attempts to use the vacuum cleaner may interfere with vacuuming.

Brooms and mops, although lacking the brute force of vacuum cleaners, also capture the interest of the toddler. These

long-handled "creatures" are pretty wild, and one-year-olds have their hands full just keeping them in check. Fortunately, parents can substitute child-size versions, and most toddlers are delighted to sweep with a little broom while mother sweeps with the big broom. Child-size vacuum cleaners, carpet sweepers, and lawn mowers serve a similar purpose.

Any cleaning job that involves water is appealing. One-year-olds are intrigued by the way a sponge soaks up water and are delighted with the task of sponging off the kitchen counter or table top. They enjoy polishing a mirror with water or mopping up spills with a damp cloth. Helping to wash the car is an extra-special cleaning job that can be the high point of any toddler's day.

PLAY IDEAS

We have discussed three common types of housework, although there are numerous other jobs around the house that toddlers observe and want to try. They see clerical jobs such as typing, paying bills, licking stamps, and mailing letters; gardening jobs such as planting, weeding, harvesting, and mowing the lawn; construction jobs such as sawing, hammering, and painting; and a variety of fix-up jobs. They watch festive jobs, such as carving the pumpkin at Halloween, trimming the Christmas tree, or lighting the Menorah candles.

Each of these occasions, and many others, presents a challenge to the parents of a one-year-old. Is there a way, parents ask themselves, that I can support my child's desire to imitate and be more grown-up, and still get the work done? Perhaps, as with folding and putting away the laundry, your child can be given a small piece of the job to perform. Perhaps, as with cooking, you can find an exploratory activity that appears to be relevant but does not really interrupt your work. Perhaps you will have to accept the fact that some jobs cannot be satisfactorily completed when an interested toddler is looking over your shoulder.

Toddlers work slowly and inefficiently, and if you are rushing to complete a job, you are likely to feel frustrated. If, on the other hand, you have the time and are not terribly finicky about doing a perfect job, one-year-old help may be welcomed. Most parents settle on a middle position. They involve their toddler in housework that both parent and child can enjoy, then save the more hazardous and complicated jobs for times when the child is not around.

Whatever options you select, think through the pros and cons ahead of time. The inconvenience involved in working with a one-year-old may be considerable, but the rewards can be even greater. You and your toddler will experience a special kind of intimacy while working together. As you demonstrate a new skill, you will see your child's determined effort to imitate, and when the task is done, you will share in your child's feeling of accomplishment.

Indoor Jobs

Cleaning the House

Many one-year-olds want to help run the vacuum cleaner. Vacuum cleaners do make fine playthings, assuming you can supervise a toddler who is playing with one. When you want to get something accomplished with the vacuum cleaner, however, you probably will need to find an alternative activity for your child. Some children are happy to imitate with a toy vacuum cleaner. Another possibility is to give your child a different piece of equipment. A feather duster and a child-size mop are both suitable for toddler helpers.

One-year-olds are fascinated with squirt bottles although they may not be able to squeeze the trigger until they are almost two. Because most squirt bottles contain caustic or poisonous liquids, your child's participation is necessarily limited. If your child can operate a squirt bottle by herself, you might give her a bottle that has been rinsed out well and filled with plain water. Then, while you use the chemical cleaners, your child can clean with water.

Dishwasher Help

Loading the dishwasher is another adult job that intrigues toddlers. If you are using plastic dishes, your child's help poses no problem. If the dishes are breakable, the situation is different. Some parents show their toddler how to put silverware in the dishwasher while they handle the glasses and dishes themselves. Other parents encourage their one-year-old to work on a related cleaning job, such as wiping off the counter or a highchair tray. Try asking your child to sit on the kitchen floor and wipe off the placemats while you load the dishwasher.

Kitchen Chores

Virtually all toddlers like to throw trash and garbage in a wastebasket. You can extend this picking-up behavior in many ways. Perhaps your child is able to help clear the table, bringing leftover food and dirty dishes to the kitchen counter. This works best, of course, if you have non-breakable dishes.

Laundry Tasks

Doing the laundry is a cleaning job that permits a high level of toddler participation. Putting dirty clothes in a hamper is much like throwing trash in the wastebasket. Standing on a sturdy chair, with you right beside her, your child may want to transfer the clothes to the washing machine or, at a later point, pull them out of the dryer. Some toddlers help put clean clothes in drawers or linen closets.

Keeping Order

Perhaps your family has a special spot for coats—such as a big chair by the front door—or a collection point for shoes. Your one-year-old will enjoy keeping these hard-to-find clothes in order.

Chef at Work

Cooking with a toddler nearby can be hazardous. Minimize this danger by encouraging your child to play in a safe spot in the kitchen. Younger toddlers are still fascinated with pots and pans, and they like to investigate kitchen cupboards. You might choose one cupboard that is not in the area of the stove and open it for investigation only during cooking times. Another possibility is to purchase a set of magnetic decorations for your

refrigerator and reserve them for cooking times. When you are ready to cook, take the decorations out of a drawer and let your toddler play with them.

When you are mixing food at a counter, your toddler can sit on the counter and watch from a safe distance. Giving her a whisk or spoon will help her feel a part of the action.

Tearing lettuce for a salad is a safe cooking activity for a one-year-old. Naturally you will have to demonstrate at first, but soon your child will be able to do this job independently while you chop the other ingredients.

Make peanut butter dough (two tablespoons of peanut butter to one tablespoon of non-fat dry milk and a half teaspoon of honey). Flatten the dough with a rolling pin. Your child will join in the eating as well as the making.

Outdoor Jobs

There are a variety of outdoor jobs in which toddlers like to participate, such as: washing the car, mowing the lawn with a toy mower, and watering outdoor plants with a sprinkling can.

CHAPTER 7

Going Out in Public

The Scene: Mother is shopping in a grocery store while Allen, a twenty-one-month-old toddler, fidgets in the front seat of the cart.

Allen (in a loud determined voice): "Down."

Mother (attempting to distract Allen): "Look over there. See the pretty stack of toilet paper rolls?"

Allen: "Down, down, down!"

Mother: "Okay, you can help Mommy push the cart. Not too fast, now."

Allen: "Allen push." (At this point, Allen drives the cart into the toilet paper tower, and the whole stack comes tumbling down.)

Mother (obviously flustered): "Oh, no, Allen! I told you to be careful. Now you've got to get back in the cart."

The rules of behavior change when people go out in public. Adults try to be on their best behavior, and interaction tends to be somewhat formal and restrained. One-year-olds, of course, have little understanding of this fact of life. For them, public outings are new experiences that produce strong feelings. A child who is basically timid may be overwhelmed by the fast pace of a shopping excursion. The child's reaction to this over stimulation is to whine, cling, and insist on being carried. A more adventurous child, like Allen, can create the opposite kind of problem, refusing to sit quietly in a grocery cart or stroller.

Feelings both of excitement and anxiety are to be expected from one-year-olds in public. Although neither fits the self-controlled, polite mode that is the adult norm, parents can

learn to adapt to their child's public style. Gradually they learn how to comfort an anxious toddler or calm down an over-exuberant one. Even a child who is determined to have some forbidden thing or get into something that is off limits can often be distracted. One-year-olds are genuinely interested in new people and places, and, therefore, public outings with toddlers can turn into positive experiences most of the time.

RIDING IN THE CAR

The starting point for an excursion is generally a trip in the car, and the first potential problem is strapping the toddler into a car seat. Children tend to dislike being restrained, and particularly dislike being in the back seat. When it comes to sitting in the car seat, there cannot be a compromise.

Once your child is strapped securely into the car seat, the problem is to keep him contented. Fortunately for parents, the movement of the car puts many toddlers to sleep. Other children are quieted by a snack they can hold in their hands or a toy that is tied to the car seat. Make sure to choose a snack that your child cannot choke on.

At some point during the second year, children develop an interest in looking out of the car window. They may be mesmerized by the moving landscape, staring out of the window without making a sound. They may play a more active role, searching the scene for familiar sights and shouting excitedly when a landmark comes into view. Brian was interested in looking for McDonald's; Kori hunted for garbage trucks; Benjamin, for no obvious reason, shouted "Wa-Wa" whenever he saw a Chevron sign. Parents can extend this kind of game by pointing out objects to their children. Unfortunately, the object is often out of sight by the time the child looks in the right direction.

The most relaxing, enjoyable, and fail-safe system for amusing toddlers in a car is to sing a song. Car rides and toddlers' memories both lend themselves to songs that have repetitive refrains and verses that go on forever, such as "Old McDonald Had a Farm." McDonald can have a clock that ticks, a tiger that roars, a church bell that clangs, or an engine that goes "vrumvrum." A cassette tape of familiar songs is an acceptable substitute for a sing-along parent.

THE ISSUE OF SECURITY OBJECTS

Many a trip with a toddler has been delayed on account of a security object. A favorite blanket is in the washing machine, or a dearly loved rabbit was last seen in the kitchen. Parents are usually tolerant and even amused by a young toddler's attachment to a special toy or object. But as the child approaches two, many parents have mixed feelings, especially if the object has to go on every outing. The search for the dearly loved rabbit grows tiresome, and return trips to the grocery store to retrieve a tattered blanket can precipitate a family squabble. Bottles and pacifiers are especially troublesome. On the surface, parents express concern about their children's teeth. A more basic concern is the meaning they attach to their child's behavior. "If my child needs a pacifier and his 'blankie' every time we go to the store," parents wonder, "does this mean that he's insecure and I'm an inadequate parent?"

Parents, of course, have the option of making sure that security objects are not taken on public outings. They can insist that such objects remain in the car, or they can refuse to let children take them on trips in the first place. Before adopting such restrictions, however, parents need to consider whether their child will act any more grown-up in public without security objects. Much of the time children cannot predict who they are going to meet or what is going to happen next in a public situation. The strangeness of the situation understandably creates some feelings of insecurity. One-year-olds without security objects in hand (or mouth) may look more mature at first glance, but it is doubtful that they actually feel more secure. In fact, it is likely that a child feels most confident and outgoing when he is supported by his security object.

If parents are bothered by the sight of a pacifier in the mouth of their one-year-old, or if they think it is time for the child to stop drinking a bottle in public, they can encourage their child to substitute other security objects. Dolls and stuffed animals are traditional favorites. As children grow older, these objects provide better companionship than a pacifier or a blanket, and they are more acceptable to adults. A one-year-old who is beginning to recognize the characters on "Sesame Street," for example, may adopt a Muppet® doll for public outings. Or the child might form an attachment to a stuffed animal that resembles a character in a storybook. Some one-year-olds on public outings enjoy taking along accessories such as a purse, a set of keys, jewelry, hats, or sunglasses. In time, this kind of object may serve a security function. Other one-year-olds express a desire to carry along toys. By responding to the interests of their children, parents can suggest toys that promote new forms of play while providing emotional support.

LIMITING EXPLORATION IN A STORE

One-year-olds often feel insecure in public, but they also like to explore new territory. At a store, your child may want to handle the merchandise and venture down the aisles by himself. Instead of worrying about the use of security objects, most parents become concerned about how to manage their child's exploration. In fact, shopping in a store may turn into a new kind of game for a one-year-old. He runs away and his parents chase him. He hides and his parents find him.

As frustrating as such moments can be for parents, they are a sign of growth. Their child wants to be involved in what is going on. Sooner or later parents find themselves helping their child define an active role that is acceptable. Whether this process takes place sooner or later depends on several factors. How often is the child taken on public outings? How urgent is a child's desire to explore in public? Is the child able to climb out of a stroller or shopping cart?

Perhaps the most important variable is the pattern that has already been established at home. If a child is permitted to ex-

plore most objects at home, he will want to touch and handle things in a store. Parents may wish that their one-year-old was an active explorer at home and a circumspect shopper in public, but it usually does not happen that way. Encouraging exploration at home means that parents have to work harder supervising their child in public.

Some parents avoid the problem by not taking their child to stores at all. Other families include two parents on shopping trips. One parent does the shopping and the other watches the child. For most parents, however, these options are not available. Parents need techniques that take into account the desire of one-year-olds to be more active while at the same time permitting shopping to be completed with a minimum of hassles.

Perhaps the most common technique is to stimulate visual exploration. When one-year-olds are busy looking at things, they may be willing to stay in a stroller or shopping cart. In a grocery store, the shopping cart is moving most of the time and children are seated high enough to see all the shelves. Pointing out the variety of interesting sights as they pass by will hold the children in their places relatively well. At a mall, where children are seated in strollers low to the ground, and where the strollers stop for extended periods, children grow restless more quickly. Parents can try to alleviate this boredom by parking the stroller in a spot with a good view, such as a window, a mirror, or a spot where the child can watch other children play. While waiting for a sales clerk, parents can hold toddlers on the counter if the store permits it. From this vantage point, children can watch while the salesperson boxes or bags the merchandise and "borrows" a credit card.

The chances of keeping children in a stroller or shopping cart are even better if looking is supplemented by touching. Again, the grocery store provides the best examples. Children can eat while they sit in the cart. In fact, what could be more natural when surrounded by every imaginable kind of food?

One-year-olds can be given certain foodstuffs to hold on their laps, or they can drop these items in the back of the cart. They can hold a shopping list or a deli number. There are many opportunities to touch and hold objects at the checkout stand despite the presence of items that parents do not want to purchase. A toddler can help put food on the conveyor belt, hand money or coupons to the clerk, carry a bag with special food in it, or hold a new magazine that is being purchased.

Eventually of course, children will insist on getting out of the stroller or shopping cart. After all, everyone else in the store is free to walk around and investigate. However, even when children reach this point, sometime between the ages of one and three, the stroller or shopping cart can be used to structure their exploration. Instead of confining children inside the stroller or shopping cart, parents can encourage them to take over the job of pushing these vehicles.

First attempts at steering are not without peril. One-year-olds do occasionally crash into a display of merchandise or into another shopper. But it is much easier for parents to supervise children who stay with a stroller or shopping cart than children who roam footloose and fancy-free. In the grocery store, the shopping cart is an integral part of the shopping process and, therefore, its driver becomes integrated into the process as well. Similarly, in a department store a stroller can become part of the shopping process. Children can be allowed to put purchased merchandise in the stroller.

This strategy can, of course, backfire. Children end up putting unwanted items in the stroller, and they are opened or torn up before they get back on the shelf. Kyle's mother found that it cost her five dollars to get a thirty-five cent birthday card. A less costly alternative is to encourage a one-year-old to take a doll or stuffed animal to the mall and give it a ride in the stroller. After pushing for a while, the child often gets tired and is willing to sit in the stroller for the rest of the shopping trip.

SHOPPING RITUALS

When parents and toddlers go shopping together on a regular basis, they are likely to develop a routine. Shopping is a routine most of the time. Parents and children often discover looking and touching opportunities that become part of the routine. Jessica, at fifteen months, was fascinated by a bird mannequin in one of the stores at the shopping mall. Recognizing her fascination, Jessica's mother made a visit to the mannequin the high point of going shopping. Whenever Jessica began to get restless, Jessica's mother would say, "Oh, it's almost time to see the pretty bird." Other shopping rituals that parents described to us included a ride on a mechanical horse, a visit to a store window with a giant Raggedy Ann doll, and a trip up and down an escalator.

Shopping rituals are compromises. They are a way of accommodating the interests of the child, while giving the parents time in between to get the shopping done. Of course, one-year-olds hardly comprehend the contractual nature of such bargains, and parents can have difficulty convincing them that a ritual must come to an end. Children who have come to enjoy a shopping excursion will want the fun to go on forever.

Some parents seek a happy conclusion by holding up one finger and telling the child "one more minute." Even though the child does not know how long one minute is, this advance warning may make the ending more acceptable. Other parents capitalize on the power of waving "bye-bye." When it is time to go, they tell the child to wave "bye-bye" to whatever is being left. Parents can try to end a shopping ritual through distraction and humor. A new idea can be introduced, calculated to attract the child's attention and to facilitate a quick departure. For example, a parent might end a ride on a McDonald's merry-go-round by saying, "Now let's go outside and look for the moon," or "Let's go home and give your teddy bear some milk. He is very thirsty."

MANAGING YOUR OWN EMBARRASSMENT

When there is parent-child conflict in public, for whatever reason, parents tend to react in one of two ways. Either they hustle the children out of the store, often carrying them in their arms, or they punish the children more severely than is their custom. In a word, parents panic. They overreact because they are embarrassed. Often they assume that other adults are watching them and making critical judgments.

The truth is that other adults generally pay little attention to a one-year-old who is having a tantrum. Many of the shoppers have had the same experience with their own children and realize that such behavior is not unusual. The onlookers also have other matters on their minds. In general, their response is neutral but sympathetic. A minority of onlookers may make negative judgments, and unfortunately they are the ones most likely to voice their sentiments. Parents, being in an agitated state, wrongly conclude that these disapproving glances or critical comments represent the majority's opinion.

Feelings of embarrassment are perhaps most likely when a toddler is taken to a restaurant. In many restaurants, children are expected to stay in their seats, to talk in hushed tones, and to wait patiently for the meal to be served. Toddlers who don't mind staying still may have little difficulty with these rules, but children who like to move around are going to be fussy and restless. Surrounded by other adults who are enjoying a leisurely dinner, parents find themselves getting tense and angry.

Some parental feelings of embarrassment and anger are to be expected when a one-year-old is taken to a fancy restaurant. Many parents stay with family restaurants or fast food spots until their children are older. Other parents take along a restaurant pack with favorite toys, a book, or perhaps a snack to help with idle time. Timothy's parents made a point of talking to the diners at the neighboring table before sitting down. "This is our boy, Timothy," his father would say "I hope he is not going to bother you." Prepared for some over-exuberance, the neighboring diners became friendly and helpful, and Timothy's parents could usually enjoy a peaceful dinner.

No matter how inventive parents are in finding ways to make public outings pleasant, adults act differently in public than at home, and children pick up the difference. On the one hand, parents are more lenient. They will carry a whining child or respond to a groundless temper tantrum. On the other hand, the behavioral rules are more stringent. Children cannot go whooping through the supermarket, sing a raucous song in a restaurant, or rearrange the display in a dress shop.

A particular problem expressed by one parent was trying on clothes. When James's mother went into the dressing room and closed the door, James would escape underneath it. This was a particular problem when James scampered off when she was half undressed. One strategy she came upon was to go clothes shopping in stores that had a dressing room without an escape hatch. A second strategy that worked some of the time was to get James involved in the dressing process. "Here, James, put my jeans on the chair." "Help me take off my shoes," or "Pull down my jersey." Children, like James, who have had to endure being dressed by a parent are sometimes quite happy to turn the tables.

Fortunately, both parents and children learn to adjust to the special demands of a public outing. Exploratory children accept the extra restraint, knowing that their parents will give them some extra attention. Timid children adjust to the added insecurity, knowing that their parents are always there to keep them safe. Parents become more tolerant of a young child's public behavior and are less likely to be embarrassed by outbursts or indiscretions. As parents relax, so do their children, and the balance between tension and enjoyment that characterizes a public outing tips to the side of enjoyment.

PLAY IDEAS

Going out provides opportunities for parents as well as children to learn new things and improve coping skills. Parents constantly need to find creative ways of keeping their toddler safe and happy in his expanded universe. They are also learning ways of coping with their child's misbehavior. As he explores, he asserts his will or acts up in public. Children learn how to behave in public and how to cope with inevitable frustration when "don't touch" rules are enforced, or when they have to wait and do nothing. In Play Ideas we describe some techniques that parents can use to maximize the fun and minimize the stress of taking their toddler to public places.

At the Store

Checking Out

The check-out counter is every parent's nemesis. Not only do you have to wait in line, but the area is crowded with last minute temptations, most of which you will not want to buy. Often, however, there is some small item that you would not mind purchasing. Before you reach the check-out counter, make your decision and tell your child that now it is time to get a magazine, a package of gum, or whatever. Then encourage your child to hold this item and hand it to the cashier. Soon he will anticipate having this job. If you decide not to get anything at the check-out counter, hand your child a foodstuff from the grocery cart and ask him to give it to the cashier.

Counter Seat

One-year-olds have a habit of running away while you are waiting at a counter. You can keep your child contented and close at hand by holding him on the counter. From this new vantage point, he will see interesting things and be in a position to interact with other adults. (Some stores do not permit toddlers on the counter.)

Shopping Pal

An older toddler who wants to imitate you will enjoy shopping with his own shopping bag. Simply carrying such a symbol of consumerhood will be sufficient at first. It is possible, of course, that your child will start to fill the basket with items. You can preempt this option by giving your child some merchandise you have selected.

Treasure Hunt

Turn your shopping expedition into a treasure hunt. "We need to buy bananas. Let's see if we can find them. Do you suppose they are down this aisle? Oh great, you found the bananas. Can you help me put them in the cart?"

Stroller Push

When your child no longer will accept sitting in the stroller on shopping trips, encourage him to push the stroller instead. Putting a doll in the stroller and talking to your child about taking care of the doll makes the job more realistic and appealing. You still will be directing your child this way and that, but your comments will seem more like those of a companion than an authority figure.

Rest Stop

Intersperse in your shopping routine with a few brief activities that are strictly for your toddler's benefit, such as making a regular visit to an enticing display.

At a Restaurant

Breakfast Outing

If you like to go out to eat but fear your toddler will be a pest, try breakfast at a restaurant. The atmosphere is more casual at breakfast time, and your child is likely to be both hungry and refreshed.

Restaurant Snacks

When you go to a restaurant where there will be a delay before the food is served, bring along appetizers for your toddler. Try finger foods that encourage your child to eat slowly. For example, place a handful of cereal-o's in a row so that your child will pick them up and eat them one at a time. Give him a little box of raisins which he can fish out on his own.

Finger Plays

Finger plays are a good way to keep your child occupied while waiting to be served. The following jingle, which can be sung while sitting at the table, allows for some creative variations. (Make the rabbit with your hand by holding up two fingers for the ears.)

> *Rabbit is coming with a hop, hop, hop.*
> *He's hopping on my hand and he will not stop.*
> *He's hopping on my thumb and my finger too.*
> *Hop away Rabbit I've had enough of you!*
> *(On my shoulder and my tummy too, etc.)*

MAKING CONNECTIONS

Introduction

~~~~~~

A major development in the toddler years is the emergence of a sense of identity. Toddlers recognize that they are people in their own right, with the ability to make decisions, to make things happen, and to have an impact (both good and bad) on other people. They discover the fun of teasing and the power of the words "no" and "bad mommy." At the same time, they are delighted with applause and love to be the center of attention.

While parents delight in their toddler's new sense of self, they may also find it confusing. Why does Jessica cling to my hand when she hears a clap of thunder, but refuse to hold my hand when we walk on the sidewalk? Why does Annabelle love to play with her food, but refuse to dip her fingers into the finger paint? Why does Wade want to do everything by himself, but acts completely helpless when I ask him to pick up his toys? Why does Alicia say "love you daddy," when she wakes up in the morning and "hate daddy," when he won't let her play with a knife?

Although toddlers continue to keep us guessing, their confusing behaviors can often be explained by ambivalence about separation from their parents. The downside of discovering that you are a person in your own right is a feeling of loneliness and separation. Toddlers want to make their own decisions, assert their desires, and value their newfound ability to make people do their bidding. At the same time, they are desperately afraid of separating from the people that matter the most.

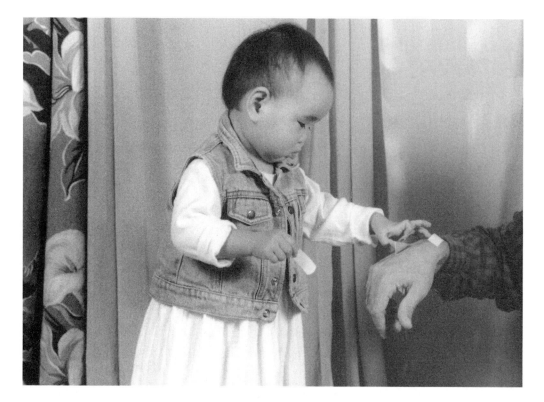

In this section, our focus is on how toddlers can balance their drive toward independence with their need to stay connected to other people. Everyday Feelings describes the range of emotions that toddlers experience and the ways in which these emotions are expressed. Word Power describes ways in which children use their developing language skills to communicate their desires and ideas. Making Friends focuses on the way toddlers initiate and maintain friendships with adults and other children.

CHAPTER 8

Everyday Feelings

The Scene: With Daddy in the kitchen.

Kathleen (pulling at the refrigerator): "Milk."

Daddy: "Good talking. I'll get you milk. Here's your cup of milk."

Kathleen (holding cup while trying to climb on kitchen chair, spills milk): "Uh-oh."

Daddy: "'Uh-oh' is right. Now you help Daddy wipe it up. This time Daddy will give you milk after you're sitting in the chair."

Kathleen (now sitting in the chair, spills the milk deliberately): "Uh-oh."

Daddy: "No. Kathleen, that was naughty. You don't spill milk on purpose."

Kathleen (in a questioning voice): "Daddy mad?"

Underlying the hustle and bustle of family life with a one-year-old is a whole range of shared emotions. In fact, the interplay of feelings between a parent and toddler is the most central characteristic of their daily routine. Each one is adjusting to the temperament and personality of the other, and the attachment bond, which was formed during the child's infancy, takes on new dimensions. In a manner of speaking, you and your child are growing both closer and further apart.

In describing the range of emotions that your toddler may be demonstrating, we identify negative emotions that challenge parents and positive emotions that delight them. We also describe two challenges that many toddlers face: separating from a parent and accepting a new sibling.

RESISTANCE AND TEMPER TANTRUMS

For many parents, the change in their toddlers' emotional tone that both surprises and concerns them is the appearance of defiance. In a predictable fashion, one-year-olds begin to say "no" during the second half of the second year. With this one small word, children discover that they can resist any suggestion or directive. Actually, there probably have been nonverbal signs of resistance for some months. Young toddlers know how to emphatically reject a bite of food by pushing the spoon away or turning their head, or how to resist being held by stiffening their bodies. The ability to resist with language, however, opens up a new vista, and for several months it may seem that the

child can think of nothing else. "No" becomes an automatic response to almost every question or request.

It is frequently difficult to tell just how serious one-year-olds are when they act defiantly. Do they really mean "no," or are they just testing the limits of their newfound power? Parents usually conclude that the best strategy is to treat an outburst of negativism as casually as possible. They may offer a brief explanation to support a request, or they may make a reasonable compromise; much of the time they just proceed as if they had heard nothing.

Annoying as the toddler's negativism can be, it is also a source of satisfaction for parents. Resistance is a sign of independence, an indication that children want to do things for themselves, be their own persons. More specifically the negativism of toddlers shows that the children are becoming aware of the scope of human decision making. They are beginning to realize that daily routines are not fixed by law or nature. Routines are decided upon by individuals, and one-year-olds want to be included in the process. At first, because their understanding is so limited, children see only the possibility of resisting the decisions of others. In time, they go beyond this initial step and find other more positive ways to take part in decision making.

Between the ages of one and two, many children also display their first genuine temper tantrums. Your child may have felt angry when he was younger, but as his ability to anticipate becomes more precise, he feels disappointment more keenly. Clearer expectations mean that frustration is that much sharper. At first, with most toddlers, their feelings of anger are

directed mostly at objects. A toy is stuck behind a chair, or a puzzle piece won't go in. Increasingly, though, some of the children's anger is directed at parents: Mom won't open the refrigerator door or Dad cuts a french fried potato in half when Isaiah likes his potato left whole.

Like other forms of negativism, you will find that it is better to ignore these tantrums than to try to console your toddler. Tantrums tend to be short-lived and your toddler's mood will soon change for the better. As a matter of fact, a toddler's temper tantrum may have a comic quality because toddlers are not too adept at pounding and screaming.

Tantrums at any age are most likely to occur in the presence of trusted adults. Recognizing that the tantrum is not just taking place in a vacuum, but is directed at them, each parent responds in a characteristic way. Some parents ignore a tantrum as it is occurring, but are quick to comfort their children after the tantrum subsides. They feel that tantrums are an expression of legitimate feelings and that angry children need help in calming down. Other parents are more punitive in their reaction to tantrums. They are convinced that tantrums are a sign of a difficult child, and they want to nip this behavior in the bud. In actuality, too much attention to a tantrum, whether the attention is positive or negative, is likely to be counterproductive. Although it may be difficult to be consistently casual when your child is screaming, it is probably the most effective method of reducing the recurrence of tantrums.

FEELINGS OF PRIDE

The tantrum behavior of a one-year-old is the negative side of a one-year-old's emotional growth. On the positive side, a new sense of independence and social power is expressed in feelings of pride. Young toddlers proudly bring objects they are investigating to parents. They want to share their sense of discovery. Older toddlers, who are more verbal, ask parents to watch them perform new tricks.

For the most part, toddlers are aware of becoming the center of attention and play the role to the hilt. If an antic such as spinning in a circle attracts adult attention, a toddler is quick to perform her repertoire. She may run up to an adult with an expectant laugh, stamp her feet in a version of a tap dance, or stick her head between her legs as the starting point of a somersault. If the adult responds to these feats with applause, the toddler is quick to join in.

One-year-olds are not insensitive to compliments either. Many one-year-old girls take special pride in donning a new

dress or a collection of costume jewelry. And many one-year-old boys puff out their chests or flex their arms in demonstrations of muscle power. Children of both genders seize opportunities to demonstrate their "smartness." Although controversy abounds over whether these traditional patterns can or ought to be changed, the ability of one-year-olds to develop feelings of pride is incontestable.

HELPING CHILDREN COPE WITH FEAR

Children who like to explore new territory and make new discoveries may be frightened when they encounter a giant-size unfamiliar character, like Santa Claus in a store or a Mickey Mouse in an amusement park.

Often parents attempt to alleviate fears by saying, "Don't worry, Pinocchio doesn't bite," or "That big Easter Bunny isn't real." Most of the time this doesn't work. A more successful strategy is desensitization. If, for instance, you know your child is frightened by Mickey Mouse, play a find-the-mouse game before you go on a trip. Thumb through a Disney World catalogue or children's magazine. Say to your twelve-month-old, "Find Mickey. You found him. Should we find another one?"

When you get to Disney World your child may still be frightened, but she may also be fascinated by a real live Mickey Mouse that looks like the picture.

Many one-year-olds develop a fear of the doctor. A doctor's kit is an excellent toy for playing out these fears. Parents can help their toddler by helping her examine her doll. "Let's look in her ears." (Put the otoscope in the dolls ear.) "Your turn. You do it." Often it is useful to simply talk about the various instruments as you and your child handle them. Although your child will not fully understand your explanations, this kind of conversation helps a toddler accept medical procedures. And while it is certainly no fun to be sick, it is quite a lot of fun to pretend your doll is sick.

AVOIDING HASSLES

When your toddler first learns to make choices, she will keep changing her mind. She will choose the blue shirt, and, as soon as she starts putting it on, will change her mind and want the red shirt. You will save time and have more fun if you turn making choices into a game. "I know you want the red shirt." When she chooses the blue shirt you respond with exaggerated dismay, "Uh-oh. I was wrong. You wanted the blue shirt." Even if your child doesn't understand the words you are using, she will recognize that this is a game and not a power struggle. At the same time, she will be less likely to change her mind. It wouldn't be so much fun if you guessed right.

The best way to avoid hassles is to ward them off. Choose your battles wisely. Make up your mind ahead of time what issues you can compromise on.

HANDLING NEGOTIABLE ISSUES

Patrick's mother described her way of dealing with Patrick's demands for a cookie before dinner. "I offer him an alternative in a matter-of-fact tone of voice. When he asks me for a cookie, I say, 'No cookie. Do you want grapes or a cracker?' Then, when he whines, 'No grapes. No crackers. Cookie!' I say to him, 'I am putting some grapes and a cracker on the table. Maybe you can reach them.' It works every time. He gets so busy trying to reach the cracker that he forgets about the cookie."

HANDLING NON-NEGOTIABLE ISSUES

In some situations, such as holding your hand while crossing the street or getting into the car seat, there is no compromise. Knowing that you might be in for a power struggle, think up ways ahead of time of making your child feel in control. If crossing the street is a problem say, "Hold my hand tight to make sure I cross safely." If the car seat is a problem, let your child choose a tape to listen to in the car. Say, "We have to hear the music, so let's see how fast we can get into the car seat." She may not understand all your words, but she will tell from your matter-of-fact tone that getting out of the car seat or not holding hands is a "no compromise" issue.

EMPATHY

In talking about special moments with a toddler, parents often describe an incident where their toddler showed an amazing capacity to empathize.

Scene: Mother and Benjy waiting at the door as Dad gets home.

Mother: "I'm so glad to see you. I had a miserable day at the office, and my head is about to split."

Dad: "Sounds like you need some quiet time. Why don't Benjy and I go pick up some pizza and you lie down for a bit."

Benjy comes out of the kitchen holding a Mickey Mouse Band-Aid®.

Benjy: "Me fix mommy," placing a Band-Aid® on her hand.

Benjy's concerns about his mother's headache is a clear example of a toddler's new capacity to empathize. The empathy of the toddler is very different from emotional outbursts of an infant who starts to cry when he hears other infants crying. Toddlers, like Benjy, not only have the capacity to recognize the sadness or pain of another person, they also seek out ways to make other people feel better. They may bring their teddy bear to a parent who is teary or offer to kiss a parent's thumb that has been smashed by a hammer.

While the empathy of a toddler is certainly an indication of expanding emotional capacity, it can also be quite confusing. Toddlers quite often will inflict pain and immediately seek to make amends. Following the Band-Aid® incident, Benjy pulled the puppy's tail and patted him lovingly when he whimpered. As toddlers increase their ability to recognize the feelings of others, they are quite likely to both cause feelings of distress and try to make amends.

SEPARATION

Both expressions of anger and resistance and expressions of pride and empathy signal an emerging self-awareness in one-year-olds. Children start to grasp the idea that they are distinct individuals. No longer do they cry automatically when other children are hurt, or become afraid when Mommy washes her hair. Space is opening up between their own experiences and the experiences of others. While this space permits a new level of independence, it also raises the specter of separation. A one-year-old who lets you know her wants in no uncertain terms, and who proudly demonstrates new skills, is also likely to express fear of separation, even when separations are brief.

Separation, in various degrees, is an everyday experience for all toddlers. At home, you will see your child gaining the confidence to explore further and further on her own. Suddenly you realize that your child has wandered into an adjoining room and is playing happily by herself. For the first time, she ventures upstairs unaccompanied and goes to her bedroom to find a toy. In these new situations, you and your one-year-old work together to define an acceptable level of separation. You want to keep an eye on what your toddler is doing, just as your toddler wants to be assured that you are easy to find.

Separation also occurs at bedtime. In fact, the way parents handle bedtime is a good indication of their general approach to separation anxiety. Some parents make a special effort to settle their child before bedtime by initiating "goodnight" rituals. When leaving their child with a baby sitter, these same parents go to extra lengths to explain separation in a reassuring way.

Other parents, who encourage their child to go to bed without fanfare, treat baby sitter situations in a similar manner.

For many one-year-olds, child-care placement represents the most traumatic form of separation. It is not unusual for children to go through several difficult months of adjustment, particularly if they have spent the first year of life in a home setting. Parents can help by maintaining a consistently firm but calm attitude toward the child-care placement. They can allow toddlers to take security objects with them to child-care. (Unfortunately, many child-care centers have a rule against this.) Parents can reassure their toddler by greeting the caregiver with confidence and enthusiasm. They can tell their child, in concrete terms, when they will return—"I will pick you up after your nap." They can make leaving less traumatic by saying goodbye in a cheerful, non-hurried, but non-hesitant way. Finally, by keeping

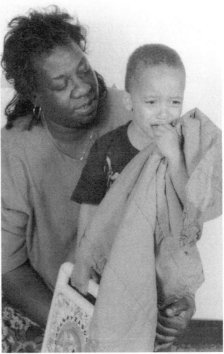

lines of communication open with substitute caregivers, parents can find out how their child is adjusting. If caregivers report, or parents observe, continued signs of depression in their child, such as withdrawn behavior or extended periods of sleeping, parents need to reexamine their choice of child-care placement.

Separation anxiety at bedtime, with a baby sitter, or at a child-care center is understandable in one-year-olds. Your child is not sophisticated enough to comprehend why you must leave her with substitutes. "If you abandon me one time," your child seems to be thinking, "might you abandon me any time?" Typically, toddlers protest vehemently when a parent leaves, but then calm down a few minutes later. Being overly responsive to the initial protest communicates to your child that the separation experience is indeed going to be frightening. Next time your child will scream even louder, and you will feel more pressure to be reassuring. Such a pattern is counterproductive for both you and your child. It cannot be reversed overnight, but if you do find yourself in this predicament, you can make a special point of encouraging brief separations in the daily routine. As you find other adults or children with whom your child is comfortable, you can arrange longer separations.

The heightened emotions associated with separation can take you by surprise. Often we hear parents say things like, "When he was a baby we would wave bye bye, and he would leave without protest. Now I can't pick up my briefcase without hearing a scream." Although we may interpret these reactions as regression, in actuality the toddler is demonstrating a higher level of understanding. He recognizes the implications of separations and is letting you know how he feels.

Ultimately, a one-year-old's awareness of separation represents a step forward and an opportunity to develop new relationships. Children expand their attachment bonds to include a wider circle of people. Friendships blossom with aunts and uncles, cousins, neighbors, older children, and peers. One-year-olds appreciate the different qualities of these new friends, and unique activities and social games come to be associated with each one. Many parents even discover that this is a good time to introduce the idea of staying overnight with a relative or adult friend. Separation can be a positive experience, a chance to feel socially independent.

No matter how you try to avoid them, situations do sometimes arise where a family cannot plan ahead for separation, or where a separation is extended. Toddlers usually react to unplanned or extended separations in a characteristic pattern. Initial crying and protestations give way to a period of acceptance when the toddler appears to be coping well. Then, when the parents return home, the toddler reacts with anger or rejection. It may take hours or even days before toddlers forgive their parents for leaving and harmony is restored. Letting toddlers see photographs of their parents, hear their voices on the phone or on a tape, and wearing some piece of clothing or jewelry that belongs to Mom or Dad may make the unplanned separation less traumatic.

THE ARRIVAL OF A NEW SIBLING

When the reason for separation is the birth of a sibling, your toddler may have an even more difficult period of adjustment. From a toddler's point of view, Mother has not only been absent without leave, but she has also returned home with a substitute baby. This new baby gets gifts from all the visitors, is the center of attention, and has no play value whatsoever. Wendy, at just under two years old, expressed her concern when first introduced to her brother: "Baby come out of tummy? Put it back!"

Fortunately, with rare exceptions, parents have plenty of time to prepare their toddlers for a big brother or big sister role. Although there is no way of eliminating negative feelings toward a new baby, parents can help with the adjustment period through advance preparation. Here are some ideas that parents have shared with us.

- Make a scrapbook of pictures of baby furnishings, including such items as a cradle, port-a-crib, crib, carriage, infant seat, diaper bag, and infant car seat. As you read the scrapbook with your toddler, talk about the things "our baby" will need.
- Take out your toddler's baby book or photo album and talk about the time when she was a baby.
- Let your toddler help sort out and fold clothes for the new baby.
- Help your toddler take care of a baby doll or a baby stuffed animal.

- Teach your toddler a lullaby to sing to the new baby.
- Let your toddler feel the new baby "pushing" in your uterus. (Avoid talking about the baby kicking. Toddlers don't like babies who kick their mothers.)

In many different ways, the toddler period is a time of strong ambivalence. One minute your child may be in the throes of a temper tantrum; the next minute she may be cuddling with you or playing cheerfully. One minute she insists on crossing the street without holding your hand; the next minute she whines to be picked up and carried. Your one-year-old is struggling to balance feelings of independence and dependence. For the first time in her life, but certainly not the last, she wants both the freedom of independence and the security of dependence. The long journey of growing up has begun, and your toddler is starting to map out her individual path.

Different families encourage independence in different ways. Parents may stress independence in the form of self-help skills, encouraging their child to use a spoon and fork, a toothbrush, or a washrag. They may emphasize independence by offering choices to their one-year-old: what juice for breakfast, what shirt for the day-care center, which toy for riding in the car? Parents may promote independence by allowing their child to help with adult jobs, such as washing the clothes or cleaning the house. They may take their child on excursions, such as a visit to a petting zoo, a trip to the park, or a visit with friends in the country, where she can explore on her own.

While each family seeks out ways to promote independence, parents are just as concerned with helping their child remain compliant. In some situations, your toddler is too young and inexperienced to make decisions for herself or to act independently. In these situations, you will want your toddler to let you be the supervisor. Again, each family reinforces a somewhat different pattern of dependence.

PLAY IDEAS

A major challenge of parenting a toddler is striking a balance between independence and dependence. Despite differences in philosophy, all families can succeed in communicating love to their children as they strike this balance. In this chapter, we have focused on several specific emotions, especially negative feelings that concern parents of toddlers. These emotions, which are prominent in the burgeoning self-expression of one-year-olds, do not exist in isolation. They are part of a complex web of feelings that connects family members. This connectedness begins at birth when you and your infant form an initial bond with each other. As your infant becomes a toddler, the connections multiply and diversify. Your toddler begins to understand that emotions within a family are played out in a context of belonging. Welcoming you home with a joyous smile, or giving you an unexpected hug, your one-year-old is learning how to say, "We belong together." The play ideas we suggest describe possible techniques for helping toddlers recognize and talk about their feelings, allowing you to capitalize on your child's burgeoning sense of humor to tip the balance in favor of happy feelings.

Identifying Feelings

Follow the Leader

Stand in front of a mirror with a child and play a version of follow the leader. Begin with "I'm feeling happy." (Smile and clap your hands.) Next say, "I'm feeling angry. Grump, grump." (Make an exaggerated mad face.) After a while, as your toddler watches you in the mirror, she will join your game. At the same time, she will recognize her own power to express and control her emotions.

Book Look

Read a book with your toddler with full-faced photos of children expressing different emotions. (They are available at most book stores that carry children's books.)

Naming Feelings

Talk to your child about her feelings. "You are angry because I won't give you a cookie." "You are sad because we can't find Teddy."

Talk to your toddler about other children's feelings. "That baby is crying. He is feeling sad." "Antoinette is laughing. She is happy." "Bernardo is kicking the door. He's mad."

Creating Happy Feelings

Silly Samples

Take advantage of your child's developing sense of humor. Put a ribbon on the milk carton, water the flower pattern on a place mat, or turn a picture frame upside down. Each time you do something silly, say "Oops!" Soon your child will join the game. Catching a parent making a mistake gives toddlers a feeling of power.

Got it in my Pocket

Play the familiar game of pretending to snatch your toddler's nose, ears, or toes and put them in your pocket. When your toddler laughs at your antics, she is letting you know that she recognizes you are teasing and is willing to share the fun.

Show Time

If you are with your child during the day, pay close attention to any new achievements that she is pleased about: pouring her own juice, making a jack-in-the-box pop up, or doing half a somersault. When your spouse comes home, or perhaps after dinner, announce that it is show time. Sit beside your spouse and ask your toddler to show off her new skills. Applaud with enthusiasm and gusto.

Photo Shoot

Take photos of your toddler when she has done something new or special. Put the photos in a small, sturdy picture album. As your toddler turns the pages talk about the photos. "Look, how you climbed all the way to the top of the hill." "Here you are pouring milk into the cereal."

CHAPTER 9

Word Power

~~~~~~

The Scene: Rachel, age twenty-one months, is at the playground with her mother. Nicholas, a two-year-old, arrives just as Rachel comes down the slide.

Rachel (giving Nicholas an ineffective push): "My slide."

Rachel's Mother (holding her squirming daughter around the waist): "It's Nicholas's turn, Rachel. Watch Nicholas. Good sliding, Nicholas. Now it's Rachel's turn."

Rachel (after scurrying up and down the slide): "Now Nicholas's turn."

When toddlers first learn to communicate ideas through language, words have a special fascination. Rachel was delighted with learning the words "my turn." Sharing the slide with Nicholas was perfectly acceptable when it gave her an opportunity to practice a new word.

Learning to communicate with words is unquestionably a major accomplishment of the early childhood years. Because the development of language is such an amazing feat, it is natural for parents to pay close attention to their child's progress. Every new word their toddler uses becomes a source of delight. At the same time, if a toddler is talking less then other children they know who are the same age or younger, parents are likely to feel anxious.

Toddlers learn language at different times, at different rates, and in different ways. Some toddlers talk in two-word phrases by the time they are fourteen months. Other toddlers who are also developing normally may be saying only a few

words at the age of two. Some toddlers seem to burst into language, some learn in fits and starts, while others acquire new words at a slow and steady rate. As long as your child understands language and enjoys making word-like sounds, you can be sure that your child will speak in due course.

Because all children have a spontaneous interest in learning language, you can capitalize on this interest in everyday interactions with your child. Some parents try to encourage speech by constantly quizzing their child—"What does the dog say, you know, tell me"—or by correcting their child—"Just say dog, not doggie." Most parents realize that the best way to encourage language is to expand on their child's spontaneous words, speak in short sentences, and include their child in a give-and-take conversation.

Toddler: "Ball."
Parent (looking in the toy box): "Yes, your ball is in the toy box."
Toddler: "Uh-uh."
Parent: "Oh, your ball is stuck in the box. Do you want me to take it out?"

Even a toddler's contribution to the conversation is only an interested stare, the free and easy prattle of his parent is an impetus to learning language.

Once children begin the process of learning language, they may expand in several ways. Some children tend to be name callers. Before putting words together, they learn the names of all the things and people they know. Other children are phrase

catchers. They learn three or four useful phrases and then put them to use in many different situations.

Nicholas was essentially a name-calling child. At a very young age, he learned to call the car, "Vrum-vrum," his food, "Yum," and his favorite teddy bear, "bah." In his first language expansion, he experimented with using these words in different contexts. He said, "Vrum-vrum," meaning, "I want to ride in the car," "I hear Daddy's car in the driveway," or "I see a picture of a car on the back cover of a magazine." After a while, Nicholas took on the task of expanding his own vocabulary. As he read through a book with his mother, he would place his finger on something in the page and look up at his mother expectantly. His mother would obligingly give the picture a name which Nicholas would repeat. By about twenty months, Nicholas could attach a name to everything he saw. Only then did Nicholas turn his attention to the task of combining words.

Katie, who was the youngest in a family of four, had a very

different pattern of language acquisition. With the exception of the people in her environment, Katie showed little interest in naming things. She wanted to talk like her siblings. Not surprisingly, Katie mastered several phrases at an early age, which she used in a variety of contexts. "I want it," "Don't like that," and "That mine" were her first well-practiced phrases. Finally, when she needed to be more explicit about her needs, Katie added new words to her vocabulary. "I want juice, I want milk, I want my dolly."

Although children acquire language at different rates and through different routes, most children will have mastered the fundamentals of language some time between the ages of eighteen months and three years. At whatever time it occurs, sharing the discovery of language is one of the purest delights of parenting a toddler.

READING BOOKS WITH CHILDREN

Mother (opening the door for her husband): "Oh, am I glad you're home early tonight. This son of yours has been a holy terror. Here he is, he heard you coming."

At this point Andrew, age fifteen months, falls into his father's arms.

Andrew: "Dadda car. Dadda car."

Father (kissing Andrew and then placing him back on the floor): "No, young man, we are not going for a car ride. Besides, Mommy tells me that you've been a holy terror. So what did you do today?"

Mother (still a bit hassled): "Andrew pulled the leaves off the new philodendron plant, scribbled on the telephone bill, and stuffed the bathroom towels into the toilet."

Father: "Sounds like it's time for a serious father and son talk. How come you're giving your mother such a hard time?" (Father walks into the family room and sits on a large chair.)

Andrew (walking toward his father with a book in his hand): "Up, Dadda. Up."

Father: "So you want to make up, do you? Hmm, let's see, Pat the Bunny. Aren't you a little young for this risque kind of stuff?"

Mother (smiling broadly): "Looks like you two will be busy for a while. I'll go and get dinner."

When a toddler climbs up on our lap with a book in hand, mischievous antics and negative moments are immediately forgotten. All parents are quite naturally delighted with their toddler's fascination with books. Book reading combines opportunities for intimacy and cuddling with opportunities to teach. It has none of the negatives associated with many other toddler activities. It is not noisy, wasteful, or destructive, and it doesn't make a mess. Best of all, a toddler's absorption in a reading activity carries with it the promise of future scholarly interests.

Despite parental preferences, toddlers' fascination with books is neither universal nor constant. Some toddlers will have nothing to do with books at all. Others go through phases. One week a toddler will be almost fanatical about wanting a parent to read to him. The next week he will wriggle out of his parents' laps and fling the book across the room. Obviously, when toddlers are going through an "I hate reading" phase, trying to force them to read is counterproductive. However, parents can try to stimulate and prolong book-loving phases. Here are some strategies that were suggested by the families we visited.

"In our family we sit down after dinner and spend about a half hour reading. I have two small rocking chairs, one for my three-year-old and one for the baby. I put a pile of books on the floor beside each of the rocking chairs. For a while. Terry and Susie (Susie is eighteen months old) sit in their own rocking chairs and turn the pages of a book. Then both children climb up on my lap, and I help them read a story. It's a happy time of day. Of course, I guess it wouldn't work as well if I had three children instead of two."

"Michael was turned off from reading books for a long time. Then I started getting him interested in looking at pictures. I pointed out the family photos on the wall, posters in the store windows, the emblems on his T-shirts, the pictures in

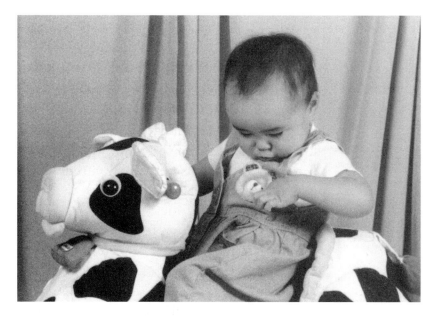

magazines, even the baby on the diaper box. I don't know if it's just coincidence, but he's back to loving books."

"Most of the time, Kathleen is too busy to sit down and read a book, but what she really enjoys is a matching game. I find the car in her book, and she runs to get her toy car. We do the same thing with a brush, doll, shoes, or spoon. I am hoping that after a while she will get interested in just looking at the pictures and naming the things she sees."

SELECTING APPROPRIATE BOOKS

Once a toddler has become interested in reading, the choice of books becomes important. Books that receive a stamp of approval from both toddlers and parents usually have at least two or three of these attributes:

- Illustrations that are bright, distinct, attractive, and not overly stylized.

- Illustrations that lend themselves to a game of hide and seek (small familiar objects are repeated on several pages).
- Illustrations that invite sound effects and encourage toddlers to participate (the cow says "Moo," or the horn goes "Beep-Beep").
- Stories about familiar topics such as animals, food, cars, and things around the house.
- Stories that describe everyday wants and daily routines. (An all-time favorite is *Goodnight Moon.*)
- Stories about "calamities," such as making a mess, breaking something, or getting very dirty. (These are especially appreciated by older toddlers.)
- Books that can be manipulated, such as touch-me books like *Pat the Bunny*, dress-up books with zippers and snaps, scratch-and-sniff books, squeeze-and-squeak books, books with tabs that make something happen, and books with stick-on characters. (Three dimensional pop-up books intrigue toddlers, but don't work very well because they are easily damaged.)
- Books that are sturdy with easy-to-turn pages.

Naturally, all of these characteristics are not always found in the same book. Parents need to stock up on the kinds of books that their own toddler enjoys most, but have other books available for variety. Some books, like some foods, can be introduced more slowly.

WAYS OF READING TO YOUNG CHILDREN

Reading a book to a toddler requires a parent's undivided attention. The sense of intimacy and togetherness that goes along

with reading a book is destroyed when a parent has to answer the telephone, turn off the stove, or respond to the needs of other household members. Although uninterrupted time is a scarce commodity in most homes, parents can try to set aside regular times to read books with their one-year-old. Once the habit is established, parents report that this reading interlude is a relaxing and pleasant time of the day.

Being a proficient reader is not really important when it comes to reading to a toddler. As a matter of fact, the most effective readers tend to ignore the printed words altogether. Children are interested in pictures, and it is up to parents to interpret the pictures in a way that the child understands. For the young toddler who is in the beginning stages of listening to a story, reading a book is like playing a game of peek-a-boo. The toddler wants to turn the pages by himself, one at a time, forwards or backwards. Then the child closes and opens the book to see the same picture again.

When a toddler wants to read a book peek-a-boo style, the best strategy for the parent is simply to label the pictures. After a while the child may be ready to engage in a game of hide and seek. "Now where's the teddy bear?" the parent may ask. "Where is the kitty who's going night-night?"

With most toddlers, hide-and-seek reading eventually leads to more active labeling. Now the children point to the pictures and proudly provide the labels themselves. At times, parents may use humor as a way of refueling their child. If a child has nothing to say about a page, the parent might mislabel a familiar object. "I see a mouse," Daddy declares as he points to a picture of a cow. "Moo-moo," the child insists, giggling at Daddy's silly error. The parent goes on, "Oh, yeah! That's a moo-moo. The moo-moo is eating an ice cream cone."

These labeling games continue to be prominent, off and on, for several years as children learn the names of unusual vehicles and exotic animals. Books that are designed for labeling, such as Richard Scary's word books, enable young children to label many objects that they have not seen (and may never see) in real life. These books also help children see more in their real environment. Having learned a new word like "bridge" from a book, a one-year-old may begin to see and point out real bridges.

As toddlers get older and become more proficient at understanding language, parents automatically change their way of reading. The labeling strategy is abandoned, and parents al-

most instinctively start paraphrasing the story by describing what is happening in the pictures. In the process, they help their children make connections between one page and another. A story about a sleeping kitty might sound like this:

"The kitty is asleep in the basket. Sh-sh. We have to be quiet, we don't want the kitty to wake up. Oh look, there's a little boy. Look, he has a drum just like your drum! Bang! Bang! Bang! He's making lots of noise. Oh, poor kitty. She's not sleeping any more. She's not in her basket. Kitty is all gone. Let's look for the kitty. That's right. Turn the page. Good for you. You found the kitty! The kitty is under the chair."

Although children's books are the most common prop for labeling and storytelling, there are many quite reliable substitutes. Any kind of magazine, catalog, or collection of greeting cards can serve as the basis of a reading experience. Of all the homemade books, the best and certainly the most popular is the family photo album. Many babies, even before they are one year old, recognize the entire family, including the cat and dog. And as the toddlers become more adept with language, they are able to identify events as well as people. The pleasure of a picnic at the beach or a trip to the zoo can be repeated over and over through a photo sequence.

TEACHING YOUR TODDLER TO READ

Many toddlers who have become avid book "readers" develop the surprising talent of identifying their books by the cover. Recognizing the fact that these children have an extraordinary memory for visual images, some parents are sold on the idea of teaching their toddler to read. Using a "sight-say" approach, they write familiar words in large letters on flash cards. Despite the enthusiasm of parent-teachers, toddlers are not likely to learn to read. With practice, some toddlers recognize a few dozen words, but being able to associate an isolated word with a flashcard is an insignificant part of reading. True reading involves comprehending the collective meaning of words that are organized into sentences and paragraphs. For a one-year-old, the best preparation for reading is the development of basic listening and speaking skills. These skills will help the child learn more about how meaning is built into language and, at the same time, provide a high level of new information for the child to process.

Simply stated, reading a word like "cat" is not an important accomplishment. What is important is talking about all the interesting characteristics of cats. And books are an excellent resource for this kind of conversation.

Books provide a powerful way to generalize first words and to expand on early phrases. Although there are many different pictures in each book, there is also a high degree of repetition. As parents and children reread books together, they search out familiar pictures in a delightful version of hide and seek. At the same time, each new reading of a book provides an opportunity to learn new words and make new discoveries. Older toddlers frequently begin to appreciate a simple story line in picture books so that reading a book turns into an imaginary experience.

PLAY IDEAS

The most significant way to help children become good readers is to instill in them, at an early age, the love and appreciation of books. In Play Ideas we describe ways of adapting reading to match the interests of different toddlers, and of making reading for all toddlers a fun and rewarding experience.

Playing With Books

Peek-a-Book

When toddlers first get interested in looking at the pictures in a book, they often focus their attention on one or two favorite objects in each book. Reading resembles a game of peek-a-boo. Your child will quietly turn the pages of a book until he finds a favorite image, then close the book and start again. Parents can hold the book in a way that allows them to share these moments of excitement with their child.

Page Turner

Toddlers are more interested in reading books when *they* turn the pages. Give your child a feeling of control over reading. Instead of asking him to label the pictures, or labeling every picture for him, wait until he points to a picture. Then respond to his initiative by labeling the picture.

Hey Diddle...

Toddlers like to label pictures, but they also like to listen to a parent tell them about the pictures. Listening skills are even more important in language development than speaking skills. One way to encourage both listening and speaking skills is to hesitate before you say certain words. Give your child a chance to finish the sentence for you. "Look at this big dog," you might say. "She goes..." Then, if your child does not respond, you can finish the sentence and continue your reading.

Photo Album

One of the most popular kinds of books among toddlers is a photo album. Your child will enjoy labeling family members and hearing you retell memorable experiences. You also can create your own picture book by putting magazine pictures in a photo album. Many children like homemade books with animal pictures. Your child may also like a book with foods, cars and trucks, or babies.

Activity Books

One-year-olds like books that have parts which can be touched and manipulated. A counting book; a scratch-and-sniff book; a book with movable, velcro-backed pieces; a book with sturdy pull tabs—these specialty books combine the fun of reading with the excitement of making something happen.

Paraphrasing

Most young toddlers would rather talk about the pictures in a book than read the story line. As your child gets older, he may show interest in listening to a story that accompanies the pictures. Even at this point, it is often best to tell the story in your own words, adjusting it to fit your child's attention span.

Word Games

Treasure Hunt

Go for a walk outside with your toddler. See how many things he can name. Truck, car, plane, dog, cat, bird, baby—the more experience your child has with seeing an object and hearing you name it, the faster his vocabulary will grow. Another effective way to encourage language is to repeat the word he has said, and then put the word in a short sentence. When your child points to a dog and says "woof," repeat the word "woof" and then add, "The dog says woof."

Name Game

As you walk with your child, talk about what you are doing. Use short phrases. We open the drawer, find a spoon, close the drawer, pick up the teddy bear, find the book, peel the banana, eat the banana. The list could go on and on. The best way to learn language is to hear it spoken in context.

Tape Recording Fun

Tape record yourself giving directions to your toddler. Here is a good sequence for bath time. "Find your toes, wash your face, pick up the soap, dry your ears." Turn on the tape and help your toddler follow the directions.

Oops!

When your toddler has learned to name familiar things, play a "mislabeled" game. Catch his toe and say "I found your ear," or hold up a picture of grandma and say, "Moo-moo, I found a cow." Your toddler will laugh at your silliness and maybe join the game.

Picture Perfect

Photographs of family members are intriguing to one-year-olds but often must be handled with care. Try giving your toddler a few photographs that he can explore on his own. Slip pictures inside a clear plastic frame or key ring. Or make a refrigerator toy by laminating a photograph and mounting a magnetic strip on the back. Still another possibility is to put several pictures in a pocket size photo album and tape the sides of the pages so that the photographs cannot be removed.

Telephone Answer

Telephone games are a perfect way to develop communication skills. While play telephones are available in almost any store that sells toys, real telephones that are unplugged and out of use make ideal props. Begin the game with one telephone. Pick up the phone and pretend to talk. "Hello Nana, are you going to the store? Goodbye." Give your toddler a turn. Next, try the game with two phones, one for you and one for your toddler.

Make the conversation short. Toddler: "Hello." You: "Nana is coming." Toddler: "Bye." When your toddler has learned telephone turn-taking, he is ready to talk on the real phone.

Puppet Play

Puppets are a natural for practicing conversational skills. While we cannot expect one-year-olds to talk for a puppet, they are perfectly happy to talk to a puppet. Begin by putting a puppet on your hand (a sock with eyes sewn on works fine) and then let the puppet ask questions, give directions, or recite a favorite ditty. When your toddler requests the puppet, give it to him, but don't be surprised if all he does is put his hand inside the sock and wiggle it around. Talking for a puppet is a complex skill that children are not likely to master until they are two or three.

CHAPTER 10

Making Friends

~~~~~~~~~~~~~~~~~~~~~~~~~~~~~~~~~

Scene: Mother, Father, and Dahlia in the living room of their home.
Mother: "I've invited a friend over for Dahlia."
Father: "Great. They'll have a fine time. Probably discuss their favorite pacifiers, or
  maybe they'll talk about the relative merits of disposable diapers."
Mother: "Oh, don't be silly. Dahlia and Timothy really do play with each other."
  (The doorbell rings.) "Here they are now."
Timothy's Mother: "I hope we're not too early. Timothy couldn't wait."
Mother: "No, come right in. Dahlia is waiting for you."
By now the two toddlers have crept up to each other and are happily tugging at each
  other's shirts.

In this chapter, our focus is on ways that toddlers make friends with adults, children, and pets. Much to the delight of their parents, Timothy and Dahlia have discovered the fun of playing with each other. Toddlers do have the capacity to initiate and sustain friendships. Expectedly, there will be some tears when there is a clash over toys or when hair gets pulled too hard. What is most amazing to parents is that toddlers are likely to play happily together immediately after an angry outburst.

Making friends with adults is not as instantaneous as making friends with other toddlers. New adults who approach toddlers with too much zest and enthusiasm, even if they are relatives, are likely to be rejected. Adults who recognize that a casual greeting and a shared interest in a toy are effective icebreakers are more likely to be accepted. Pets, like adults, can either scare or delight a child, but are most likely to be accepted if they are longtime members of the family.

MAKING FRIENDS WITH OTHER ADULTS

One-year-olds are overcoming their earlier fear of strangers, although they may still be frightened of visitors who look especially strange to them. If these adults remain friendly without being intrusive, toddlers are likely to return the friendship. One-year-olds are reassured when adults smile and talk to them, but are leery of adults who demand hugs and kisses or who bombard them with questions. Many adults, of course, have a favorite routine for winning over a young child, once

the initial ice is broken. They may cover their eyes with their hands, then open them slowly and say "peek" in a squeaky voice. They may start a finger moving in a circle, then, buzzing like a bee, move it closer and closer to the child's belly button. Or perhaps they may do a simple magic trick, such as finding a penny behind the child's ear or pretending to find something in their pocket.

The most straightforward way for adults to make friends with one-year-olds is to offer them an interesting object. The children do not comprehend many of the verbal formulas for communicating friendliness, but handing them a toy is a

gesture they understand. In fact, one-year-olds frequently signal a desire to make friends by giving an object to a visiting adult, as if to say, "Here's something for you. Do you have anything for me?" As they get older and bolder, children may actually appropriate objects that belong to an unknown adult. When the visitor puts down a purse or hat, the child reaches out to explore it.

Rather than scold your child for playing with someone else's things, you can use this curiosity to foster friendship. You might remind your toddler that permission is needed, and then help her do the asking. "Would it be all right if Matthew tried on your hat and looked in the mirror?" "Michelle is very interested in your purse. Do you have anything in your purse she could look at for a few minutes?" Naturally, you need to treat each situation separately and decide how to phrase your child's request delicately. In most instances, however, adults are more than happy to share their possessions temporarily with a one-year-old.

With older and more verbal one-year-olds, an effective way for adults to begin is with a play routine. An adult, for instance, may take out a mirror and a comb and talk to the child's stuffed animal. "Oh, Teddy, you want to borrow my mirror? You need my comb? Oh, all right, but hold on tight." In short order, the toddler will get interested in the play and forget about being shy.

One-year-olds also enjoy meeting adults outside the home. Sitting securely in the seat of a grocery cart, a toddler may suddenly greet a passing stranger. Walking in the mall, she may share a brief encounter with a fellow window shopper. Given repeated experiences with the same adults and a chance to make contact by exchanging objects, a one-year-old will develop definite friendships with clerks in stores, adults at church, and neighbors.

A parent's workplace is an environment with many possibilities for making friends. Secure in the knowledge that a parent is nearby, a child can watch a variety of new adults who have an intriguing assortment of novel objects. Over time, these faces become familiar and the objects that surround them become the focus of exploration and friendly interaction.

MAKING FRIENDS WITH OTHER CHILDREN

Toddlers play with older children and teenagers in the same way they play with adults. They explore objects with them, play with toys and books, and share physical games. Like adults, these older children are able to adjust their play to fit the interests of a one-year-old. In some ways, they are even better players than adults because they are more interested in the toys that appeal to one-year-olds. A preadolescent who regularly babysits may be a favorite companion.

One-year-olds also want to make friends with children who are only a few years older. These preschool children will

sometimes include younger children in their play. Often, however, their play is very boisterous, and the running and chasing games prove too much for the toddler. One-year-olds are left standing on the sidelines, valiantly trying to imitate bits and pieces of the fast-paced play they are watching.

A mixed-age play group offers many advantages for one-year-olds. There may be children old enough to play individually with a toddler, or children who have sufficient leadership skills to include toddlers in group pretending. There may be other children who are close enough in age to serve as models for one-year-olds. Sometimes, of course, a mixture of ages results in older children lording over younger ones and dominating their every move. But if the age range is broad and play is monitored by adults, a mixed-age group can encourage cooperation.

Despite the potential in mixed age groups, many one-year-olds are grouped with peers at day-care centers, church classes, and play groups. Traditionally, it was thought that the children did not play very well together in this kind of situation. Episodes of peer play seemed sporadic and likely to end up in a tussle over some toy. More experience with groups of one-year-olds and more careful observation have made it clear to experienced caregivers that this picture is not altogether accurate. While it is true that one-year-olds sometimes fight loudly over toys, it is almost as common for them to give toys to each other. Even when they are not playing together, toddlers spend a good deal of time watching and imitating each other. In fact, the level of interaction and sharing is surprisingly high in a group of one-year-olds who have played together for months and know each other well.

We suspect that the attitude of parents and other adults is a critical variable in increasing the peer play of one-year-olds. Usually adults adopt one of two roles when supervising a group of toddlers. Either they play directly with the children, taking the role of a stimulator, or they let the children play by themselves as long as they are not fighting. The alternative that is often overlooked is for the adults to act as facilitators of peer play, to help one child make contact with another. Perhaps by looking for opportunities to help toddlers play with each other, adults can promote a higher level of social interaction.

As parents become more attuned to the possibilities for peer interaction, they can also make changes in the physical environment. There are no hard and fast rules for designing a toddler play environment, but we have certain clues. One-year-olds interact more and share toys better when the toys are oversized. A toddler slide is a good example. It is large enough to be shared easily and actually is more fun when used by a group of one-year-olds. The children learn by watching each other and then imitating.

There are several other common situations in which large toys lead to imitative, parallel play. Older toddlers enjoy sharing a bathtub or climbing in and out of a crib. A small group may start a game by taking turns jumping off a hassock or a porch step. Well-equipped child-care settings are likely to have several oversize toys for groups of one-year-olds: a busyboard that is

big enough for several children to operate simultaneously, a large stacking toy that invites a group effort, a double-width slide, a large truck on springs, or wheel toys that have steering wheels, horns, and seats for more than one child. With smaller toys that can't be shared, child-care centers find that it is a good idea to put out two of the same toy.

According to several studies, toddlers are also drawn to each other when there are no toys at all. With only a few objects to explore, children get involved in imitating each other's body movements and facial expressions. They play peek-a-boo and chase each other. While adults would not want to offer one-year-olds an environment without toys, they can encourage this kind of play in the form of group songs. The children may not be able to sing along very well, but they can join in by moving to the music and making appropriate gestures.

We clap, clap, clap our hands,
Clap our hands together.
We wave, wave, wave our arms,
Wave our arms together.

Adults who want to try group songs with one-year-olds can buy a children's record to get started and then use their own creativity to put additional finger plays, nursery rhymes, and exercises to music.

By observing the interaction patterns of toddlers, we can discover other clues for facilitating peer play. In a home situation, parents can watch the play for a while in order to identify patterns and then introduce appropriate modifications. Allison's mother, for instance, noticed that Allison and her friend, Peter, spent their time chasing each other in a circle out of the kitchen into the dining room, around the hall and back into the kitchen. Instead of restricting their running, she decided to slow them down by creating way stations along the route. She placed a bell that could be pulled on the dining room door frame, a bean bag chair in the dining room for climbing and jumping, and a basket of hardware odds and ends in the kitchen. As the youngsters made the circuit, they frequently stopped at one of the stations, and the play went along at a leisurely pace for a surprisingly long time.

HANDLING CONFLICTS

Peer play between toddlers does not always proceed without conflict. Between the ages of one and two, children become capable of hurting each other intentionally, and intervention is a must. Adults can often remind children who are acting aggressively that it hurts to be hit or bitten. In addition, toddlers can be helped to understand the consequences of aggression by giving attention to the child who has been hurt. Then both aggressor and victim can be encouraged to make up. Perhaps the children can be induced to follow a parent's lead and touch each other. Although one-year-olds have a limited ability to solve interpersonal conflicts verbally, they do understand conciliatory body language. Parents can demonstrate this way of making amends themselves whenever an occasion arises. "Ooh, right in Mommy's eye," a parent might exclaim when her child accidentally pokes her with an elbow. "Kiss it, so it'll be all better."

Some one-year-olds develop a regular habit of pinching or biting their peers. Watching these children, it is hard to avoid the conclusion that their attacks are designed to get attention. Those they pinch and bite are often the children they like best. Naturally, this method of initiating play is unacceptable, and it can be very embarrassing for the parents of the pinchers and biters. Nevertheless, pinching and biting are not unusual among one-year-olds. Many children go through at least a brief period in which they experiment with aggressive tactics, seeing if they will lead to interesting social encounters.

Looking for a quick solution for biting or pinching, parents sometimes choose to retaliate in kind, a pinch for a pinch and a bite for a bite. The rationale given by these parents is that they want their children to realize that pinching and biting hurts. From the child's point of view, however, the lesson that is learned may be quite different: it is all right to bite and pinch as long as you are bigger and stronger. For parents who do not wish to model aggressive behavior, the alternative is to monitor peer play closely and to intervene when the child is about to pinch or bite. This approach, although it requires continuous effort, helps children learn in a positive way that biting and pinching will not be accepted.

Finally, let us close with a word about child-care. We can be sure that, in the years ahead, an increasing proportion of toddlers will be placed in some kind of child-care. It is safe to assume that the children will adjust well to this peer group setting, particularly as we become more knowledgeable about how to structure their environment. At the same time, we should not lose sight of the fact that it will be difficult for some one-

year-olds to go into a group situation. Separation fears can be expected, especially if children have spent a good part of their first year at home. The children may realize that their parents will return to pick them up, but this does not take away from the unpredictability of their day with substitute caregivers. Who will protect and reassure them in times of trouble? How will the substitute caregivers react to their moods and feelings? Until the children find out the answers to these questions, the child-care environment will seem foreboding.

Parents also look for the answers to these questions when they choose a child-care environment. They want to find sensitive, loving caregivers, who will help children feel more secure in a group situation. We would suggest that parents also look for adults who are good at facilitating peer group play. Adult attention is at a premium in a child-care setting, and the children look to each other for companionship and emotional support. Although peer group interaction is just beginning with one-year-olds, we believe that caregivers who stimulate this kind of play will make life happier for the children in their care.

BABY-SITTERS

Whether or not parent's work outside the home, they are likely to need baby-sitters from time to time. Parents who decide to use a baby-sitter, perhaps for the first time, are often unsure about how to handle leave-taking. Should I introduce the sitter ahead of time? Should I leave while my child is awake? Or should I wait until he's asleep? Should I make a point of saying goodbye? Or should I just leave?

Although there are no perfect answers to these questions, parents who use baby-sitters offer the following advice:

- Give your toddler an opportunity to get to know the sitter while you are at home.
- Tell your toddler that you are planning to go out, even if you don't think he understands.
- Have a neighbor, relative, or friend serve as a back-up if you are going any distance.
- Give your baby-sitter a list of emergency numbers, including your back-up person.
- Explain your toddler's sleep routine to the sitter.
- Get the sitter and your toddler engrossed in a game or book.
- Say goodbye quickly and matter-of-factly.
- Don't look back as you go out of the door.
- Have a good time.

MAKING FRIENDS WITH PETS

In this chapter, we have talked about how toddlers make friends. They make friends with aunts and uncles, friends of the family, baby-sitters, teachers, and children of all ages. Some of their best friends, though, are family pets.

One-year-olds can be rough on pets, and sometimes pets are too temperamental to be trusted with young children. As these photographs illustrate, however, most of the time toddlers and family pets are mutually attracted to each other.

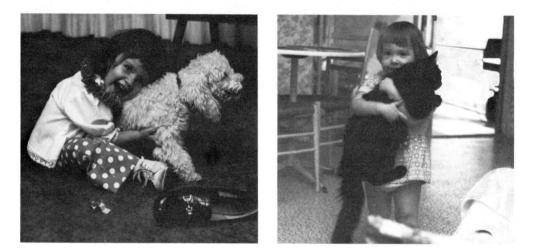

PLAY IDEAS

Of all the skills that children acquire, learning to make friends is certainly the most significant. Children who feel confident about their friend-making skills are likely to carry those skills into preschool and beyond. In Play Ideas, we suggest ways of helping children get along with peers and adults. We suggest activities that parents can try out when children come over to play.

Adult Friends

Joining the Play

If an unfamiliar adult is coming for a visit, begin a game with your toddler like rolling a ball or blowing bubbles. When the visitor arrives, immediately suggest that she join the game. Your toddler is much more likely to make friends with a playmate than with someone who gives her a hug, pats her on the head, or tells her how much she has grown.

Hosts and Hostesses

When you invite a child to the house, let your toddler help with the preparations. She can put two or three toys out that she is willing to share, or help with the preparation of a snack.

Toddler Friends

Most of the time when toddlers get together, they enjoy playing chase, emptying bookcases, or dumping toys out of the toy baskets. Sometimes this energetic imitative play can get out of hand. It is a good idea at this point to introduce a more arranged activity.

Marching Parade

Give each toddler a paper hat, a pie plate, and a wooden spoon. Turn on march music and watch the parade begin.

Wastebasket Ball

Decorate a wastebasket with a happy face drawn on newspaper. Give each child a foam ball. The toddlers will enjoy tossing, dropping, or placing the ball inside the basket.

A La Carte

Make some homemade play dough (flour, water, and a spoonful of cooking oil). Give each child a small rolling pin, plastic cookie cutters, and a tray. Watch as they prepare dinner.

HAVING FUN

Introduction

The Scene: Peter and his mother are standing on the front lawn waiting for Peter's dad to come home from work. As he arrives, Dad lunges toward Peter in a football tackle position, thrusts his head in his son's tummy, and lifts him up into the air.
Peter: "More, more." (Kicking his legs and laughing out loud.)
Dad: "All right, all right." (Sitting Peter on his shoulders.) "But first let me say hello to your mommy."

Parents enjoy playing this kind of game with their one-year-olds. We might call it an "interlude game." For a minute or two, perhaps for only a few seconds, the parent and child share a bit of roughhousing, a ritualistic game, or a private joke. The parent who hides a candy first in one hand and then in the other is subject to a stubborn search. The parent who wears a Frisbee® like a hat is rewarded with a curious smile. The parent who makes a fierce face and threatens, "I'm gonna get you," is greeted with shrieks of excitement. Children realize the absurdity in a candy disappearing, the incongruity in a Frisbee hat, and the utter unbelievability of a parent-monster.

Over the course of the second year, parents will watch their children learn how to start the silliness, too. Some jokes are stumbled upon quite by accident, but as soon as the child notices the audience's reaction, the joke is repeated and stored for future use. Many one-year-olds, for example, find that a sudden reversion to crawling brings an appreciative laugh from others. Perhaps the child gains center stage by shuffling around in Dad's shoes or by performing a half completed somersault. One-year-olds also pick up joke routines through imitation. Seeing the Frisbee on Mother's head, a toddler may be inspired to experiment with a variety of headgear, such as boxes, pans, and vegetable sieves.

When one-year-olds first discover their power to make a joke, they sometimes miscalculate. In hopes of getting a laugh, a toddler may pinch a parent's arm or run away in a store. Mischievous behavior can even become deliberately obstinate. Having discovered that pouring milk on the floor makes Mother lose her temper, the toddler seeks out every opportunity to overturn a drink. Similarly, a toddler may stubbornly continue to pull leaves off a plant, refuse kisses, or mercilessly tease a pet.

Parents who are sure their toddlers know better become convinced that their children are being mean on purpose. Usually, however, the children are only testing out the inconsistent responses of parents. All of us tend to smile indulgently when a toddler tries to tease us, but then get angry when the behavior is carried too far. It takes a few months for children to sort out these mixed messages and identify acceptable teasing routines. After a while, children recognize that getting a negative reaction from parents, impressive though it may be, is not worth the consequences. Parents go through a difficult period when their children act defiant. With a large part of their time devoted to playing policeman, parents can lose sight of the fun of parent-child play. They may forget how parent-child play nourishes feelings of togetherness.

Peek-a-boo is a universally favorite game for toddlers as well as babies. In the course of the second year, a new version of peek-a-boo arises. Instead of hiding under a blanket, Dad hides behind a chair and challenges Amelia to find him. Amelia shouts with glee as she discovers a rather large Daddy hiding behind a rather small chair. Next, Amelia takes a turn, and as you would predict, she hides behind the same chair. It is quite obvious that the baby version of peek-a-boo has turned into hide and seek. Of course, as we watch Amelia play with her parents, we recognize that the toddler version of peek-a-boo is much more elaborate then the infant version. Vigorous and rowdy toddlers like Amelia may want the game to continue when their parents have had quite enough.

CHAPTER 11

Action Games

~~~~~~

Scene: A bedroom, early morning. Dad is hiding under the sheet. Mom enters the
*   room carrying Caroline, age eighteen months.*
Caroline: "Where Daddy, where Daddy?"
Mother (placing Caroline on the bed): "Daddy's not here. Daddy went to New York
*   City."*
Daddy (extricating himself from the sheet): "Peek-a-boo—I see you!"
Caroline laughs uproariously and covers her Dad back up with the sheet.

A NEW LEVEL OF VIGOR

Now that the children are walking well and rapidly developing new physical skills to accompany walking, physical
games become more vigorous. By themselves, children may still
be rather tentative and cautious but, with the support of parents, they are transformed into raring-to-go daredevils. In
games of peek-a-boo, for example, one-year-olds enjoy stagger-
ing around the room with a blanket over their heads—bumping
into walls and furniture, falling down—until finally the blanket
is removed and they triumphantly emerge.

Lifting and swinging games, jumping routines, wrestling
matches, all sorts of physical exchanges become rougher and
more daring as toddlers get bigger. Many parents, for example,
like to lie on their backs and lift their one-year-old into the air
with their feet. Balanced on his parents' feet, the toddler swings
back and forth until he topples, usually head first into the arms

of his parent. The toddler is regularly turned upside down as he dismounts from a parent's shoulders or comes down from a brief visit to the ceiling. No longer are "horsy rides" on Dad's leg limited to gentle "Old Nellies." When Dad sings, "Watch out! You're gonna get bucked off!" he means it.

Gradually one-year-olds learn how to initiate these vigorous physical games. They are likely to sit on an unsuspecting stomach or head of a parent who is resting on the floor. A back that bends low enough to the ground is in danger of being pounced on; an outstretched leg encourages monkey bar antics. Parents who sit quietly minding their business become mountains over which to scramble. Each of these maneuvers can be the opening moves in a physical game. In a manner that is well meaning but sometimes quite sudden, the children are asking parents, "Do you want to wake up and play with me?"

One of the best arenas for vigorous physical games is the

playground. You and your one-year-old can share equipment that would be too much for a child alone. Together you can zip down a tornado slide, get dizzy on a fast merry-go-round, ride a big tire swing, or operate a full-scale teeter-totter. Your toddler experiences the thrill of danger while safely cradled in your lap.

Toddlers have a great time going swimming with their parents. From the point of view of a toddler, the reason for swimming is not to learn to swim. Swimming is a time for jumping up and down with a parent and gulping down some water. Toddlers who are young or on the timid side are quite satisfied to hold tight to their parents as they walk across the pool, or wade in a lake or a very calm ocean. Older and more adventurous toddlers dunk their heads in the water and attempt to swim or jump from the side of the pool into the arms of a parent.

A NEW EMPHASIS ON IMAGINATION

Just as one-year-olds develop the strength and coordination for a new level of vigor, they develop the mental ability to understand imaginative twists to physical games. Parents naturally talk to their children while they play and, sooner or later, they make up story lines to go along with favorite physical games.

A game of peek-a-boo, for example, fits the story line of going to sleep. "Night, night, sleep tight" the parent intones solemnly as the child is covered with a blanket. Then, as the child peeks out from under the cover, the parent acts amazed: "What? You're already awake? Okay, time to get up!" A few moments later, the parent renews the game. "Time to go to sleep."

Another common story line might be called "Anybody Home?" The child hides in the pantry and the parents pretend that they are visiting. They knock politely on the hideout door

and inquire, "Anybody home?" There may be no answer until the parents carefully inch the door open, whereupon the one-year-old occupant responds with a coy smile, a bubbling giggle, or a roar. "Oh, here's Miss Happy (or Mr. Gigglebox, or Pantry Monster)!" the parent comments with surprise.

One of the most fertile imaginary themes in physical games is monster play. The imaginary monsters that ramble through the games between parents and one-year-olds are, of course, quite benign. Frequently the parent adopts a monster role in the context of a chase game. For months, the parent has been chasing the child with the warning, "I'm gonna get you!" Now the parent feels the

need to follow through, to think of something more to do once the child has been captured. Monsters are usually hungry: the chase monster may love to nibble on the fingers, elbows, and ear lobes of a one-year-old. Despite voracious chomping and growling noises, the child recognizes such attacks for what they are: barely disguised, and very slobbery, kisses. In time, the monster may promise to eat the whole child up, or graduate to some other extravagant threat.

"I'm going to sweep up the floor." (This requires holding the victim upside down and swinging him back and forth. The parents are careful, of course, not to hit their toddler's head on the floor.)

"I'm going to send you to the moon." (This involves spinning around in a circle with the child held over your head. A parent should not play this game under a ceiling fan.)

"I'm going to throw you onto the trash heap, and you'll never, never get down." (A bean bag chair works well.)

A NEW WAY TO SHARE IDEAS

Adding an imaginative layer to physical games makes them more fun. It also floods a one-year-old's mind with new ideas. These ideas may be too exotic or mysterious to be understood right away, but they help children recognize the exciting potential of fantasy. Some physical games, on the other hand, are designed by parents to combine the fun of a game with teaching a child new words.

Physical games that require naming body parts are an effective way of expanding a child's vocabulary. If the game for today is about noses, the child and parent may take turns squeezing each other's noses, or the child may go around the room touching the nose of every available player while the parent says "nose." A body parts game can become still livelier if parents ease up on the direct instruction some of the time. They might quack or make some other unexpected noise when the toddler touches their nose. They might pretend the child has taken off the body part. "Hey, did you take my nose off? Well, put it back then."

The best physical games for teaching language involve singing and dancing. Whether parents and one-year-olds are exercising together, dancing to a tape, or marching to the beat of their own homemade instruments, they can introduce new words and make them part of the game. Kenneth and his Dad were especially fond of the "Paddywhack" song. The sillier the rhymes that Dad could think up, the more fun they had with the game: "This old man, he said crummy; he played knick-knack on your tummy." (In other verses, "smell-bow" rhymed with "elbow," "squeeze" with "knees," and "got 'em" with "bottom.")

Jennifer and her mother played an animated version of "Here We Go 'Round the Mulberry Bush." Jennifer's mother began: "This is the way we clap our hands," as Jennifer did her best to follow the movements and hum along. Additional verses involved swinging their arms, kicking their feet, and wiggling their bottoms. In a grand finale, Mother swept Jennifer off her feet and sang: "This is the way I give you a hug, give you a hug, give you a hug."

As your toddler progresses from one to two years of age, the physical games that you play together become more com-

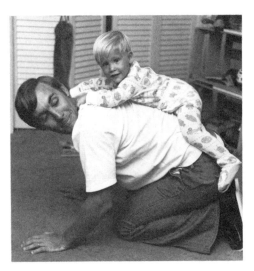

plex and involve a new level of vigor. Physical games are also expressions of intimacy, ways to extend hugging and kissing. Parents and one-year-olds look for opportunities to touch each other, and touching leads spontaneously to a game. Hands are slapped together in a version of pat-a-cake, or joined in a vigorous high five.

Arran and his mother had recently visited the zoo. Later, when Arran was playing in a favorite cupboard behind the couch, it seemed as though he was in a cage, too. Taking the cushions off the back of the couch created the illusion that Arran was actually in the zoo behind bars. He enjoyed making faces at his mother and kissing her through the bars. The game of "monkey in the zoo," begun during a moment of inspiration, delighted both Arran and his mother and soon became a featured attraction of their daily routine.

PLAY IDEAS

One-year-olds relish opportunities to engage in active play with other children, and up to a point their parents share this enthusiasm. In Play Ideas we describe a sampling of activities that are favorites in many families. Remember, spontaneity is the key ingredient in physical games. The best games for one- to two-year-olds are those on which parents and children have put their personal mark. They are games that have grown out of the spirit of the moment, when both parents and children were open to new possibilities.

Interaction Games

Thumbkin

The well known song, "Where is Thumbkin?" can be adapted to fit any body part: Where is elbow? (parent sings in tone of suspense)

Where is elbow?
Here it is! (Suddenly grabbing child's elbow.) Here it is!

How are you today, Sir?
(Gently shaking, squeezing, or tickling elbow.)
How are you today, Sir?
Are you fine? Are you fine?

High Rise

Toddlers love to be lifted high into the air. These games provide a natural way to teach words like "up and down" and "whew, am I tired." Try putting your child on your legs, lifting your legs up in the air, and saying, "Down we go, whew, I'm tired."

A parent can lift a one-year-old high enough to touch the ceiling. Maisha and her father developed a game in which Dad walked around the house with his daughter on the ceiling. But each time he came to a doorway he said, "Whoops, she's stuck again." After rescuing her by lowering her through the door, he put her back on the ceiling.

Turtle Wrestling

Wrestling is another way for parents and toddlers to play vigorously together. Kneel on the floor and put your head down, like a turtle inside his shell. Let your toddler climb and jump on your "turtle shell" until suddenly, like a volcano erupting, you rise and toss the child this way and that.

Stuffed Toy Wrestle

Hold up a toy stuffed animal. Let your child wrestle with it. In this kind of match, the toddler is the one who is bigger and stronger.

Hiding Games

Blanket Hide

Any version of hide and seek appeals to a toddler, as long as it is not difficult to find the person who is hiding. A blanket, whether on a bed or not, instantly creates a good hiding place. First the child hides in the blanket, then the parent takes a turn. It is always easy to recognize that big lump under the blanket.

Magic Game

Hiding games are fun on a smaller scale as well. Now that your child understands the permanence of hidden objects, he will enjoy simple disappearing tricks. "The penny is not in this hand, not in that hand. Hmmm, here it is in your hair!" Objects can disappear into a child's sleeve or sock, or down the front of

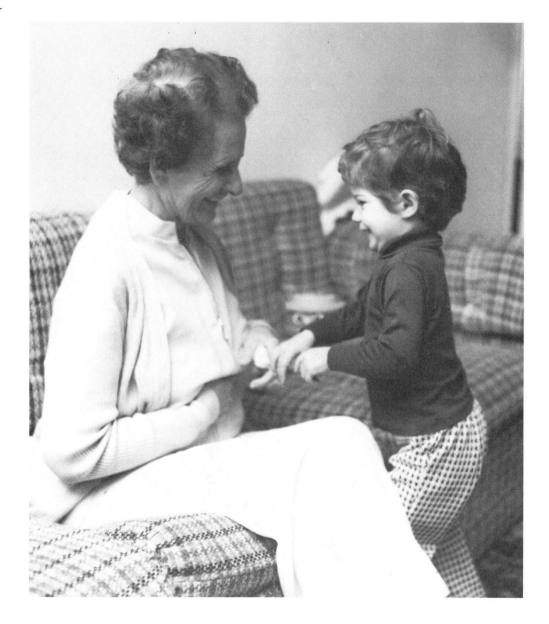

a child's shirt. One of the best magic tricks is to make something disappear into your pocket. Toddlers take great pleasure in foiling the magician and finding such objects.

Chasing and Hugging

Parents love to chase toddlers and toddlers love to be chased. In fact, the object of the game is to be caught. Your child knows that he gets a big bear hug every time you catch him.

Playing Sound Games

Megaphone Play

Many physical games involve making playful sounds. Sooner or later, parents and toddlers discover that all sorts of sounds, including whispers and normal speech, are more intriguing when broadcast through a cardboard tube. Give your child a spindle from a paper towel roll, or a tube from a roll of wrapping paper. The longer the tube, the more amazing the phenomenon. The sound, whatever it is, comes from the end of the tube and not from the person's mouth.

Animal Hunt

Creep on your hands and knees, bark like a dog and let your child catch you. Inevitably, he will take a turn creeping on the floor, barking or mooing and daring you to catch him.

Water Activities

Beach Walk

Go on an excursion to the beach with your toddler and bring a pail and shovel. The pail is a fine receptacle for shells, sand, and water. Naturally, you will find cookie and cracker crumbs mixed in the wet sand, but it's all in a day at the beach.

Towel Spread

Toddlers have differing opinions about water, especially ocean water. Some toddlers won't let you put them down in the sand, let alone take them in the ocean. With other toddlers the struggle is to keep them out of the water. If your toddler is bothered by sand or frightened by the ocean, try spreading a large beach towel or blanket on the sand a good distance from the shoreline. Engage your toddler in a sand game on the edge of the blanket. Hiding a toy or burying your foot in the sand and letting your toddler search for the toy or foot is likely to work quite well. Watching other children make ridges in the sand with a toy rake is another acceptable diversion. As your toddler becomes more comfortable with the sand, try moving the towel closer to the ocean. If on the other hand your child is too brave and is likely to run into the ocean, you will need to be a vigilant watcher, a firm hand-holder, and a quick sprinter.

Sand Dig

With the adventurous toddler, the greatest challenge is keeping him from running into the ocean. As with the timid toddler, the secret to success is engaging him in some games. Dig holes in the sand and let them fill up with water. Use the sand pail to gather shells or rocks. Smooth out a patch of wet sand and make handprints or footprints. And, of course, build an impressive sand castle for your toddler to knock down.

CHAPTER 12

Having Fun with Toys

The Scene: A telephone conversation.

Grandma: "What would you like me to buy for Anthony? I know he already has a million toys. I thought maybe he could use a new jacket or a nice warm sweater."

Mother: "Just bring yourself. We can't wait..."

Grandma: "Now, you know I'm not coming empty-handed, so you might as well tell me what he needs."

Mother: "Well, to tell the truth, he has plenty of clothes, but he's outgrowing his baby toys. He just loves balls and trucks and, you know what else? He's ready for some simple puzzles."

Like Anthony's mother, parents of one- to two-year-olds get almost as much pleasure out of a new toy as their children do. A new toy not only keeps a toddler busy and happy, it also offers fresh possibilities for parent-child play. Parents love to help their toddler complete a new puzzle or put a train set together. A carefully selected toy gives parents an opportunity to help toddlers learn new concepts and share in their feelings of mastery.

In this chapter, we focus on the way parents and one-year-olds play with a variety of toys. In particular, we look at ball play building with blocks, playing with cars and trucks, and pretend play with dolls. With each kind of play we discuss how parents can help their children develop new skills. Throughout the chapter, we stress the importance of letting children practice familiar games, invent new games on their own, and make their own discoveries.

PLAYING WITH A BALL

A ball is probably the single most popular toy for one-year-olds, for parents, or for any age. Balls do two of the most curious things: they bounce and they roll. One-year-olds realize that most objects fall directly to the ground when released. Balls, however, don't follow the rule. Instead of staying on the ground, they bounce back up, and instead of coming to rest where they are dropped, they roll off in any direction.

Because balls are so unpredictable when they bounce and roll, ball play is a natural for two people. A toddler version of fetch is a good beginning ball game. The adult throws the ball and the child chases it down and brings it back. A large ball,

like a basketball, is easy to track down, and carrying it back to the parent is a challenge in itself. Another early version of ball play involves the toddler tossing the ball to the adult from up close. The adult catches the ball and then hands it back to the child for another round of target practice. A small ball that the child can grasp easily, such as a miniature football, is a good ball for this kind of one-sided catch.

Some time between the ages of one and two, most children become interested in a true game of catch. The idea of sending a ball back and forth between two players, as pointless as it really is, makes sense to a toddler. Still, there is the problem of keeping the ball in bounds. The simplest way to manage this problem is for the parent and child to sit facing each other with their legs spread out. They can roll the ball back and forth and be reasonably certain that the ball will be trapped by their outstretched legs—unless of course it dies between them from lack of steam. A more vigorous game of catch can be kept in bounds by playing in a hallway. The ball may get beyond one of the players, but the walls of the hallway block deviant throws to the right or left. A ball court for a really wild game of catch is a staircase. The child can stand on the landing (with one parent nearby to keep the child from falling) while the other parent stands at the bottom of the stairs. Any kind of throw will reach the bottom of the stairs, where the parent retrieves the ball and pitches it back up.

Parents may be concerned that this ball play will prove destructive. There is no denying that an uninhibited game of catch inside the house can break something. Toy manufacturers have dealt effectively with this problem by producing foam balls. Parents who want to restrict indoor ball play can introduce other non-destructive balls as well. A Ping-Pong ball is harmless but versatile. It can be thrown with ease, but will not sail very far because it is so light. It is not likely to hurt anything it hits, and yet it has the lively bounce of a hard ball. Another possibility is to make balls out of newspaper. Although it is not much like a real ball (no bounce, no roll), it is fun to squash and mold the newspaper and then throw it into a receptacle. This is the well-known basketball game practiced in offices throughout the country. What these balls lack in quality they make up in quantity, for a single day's newspaper provides enough material for a whole basket-full of balls.

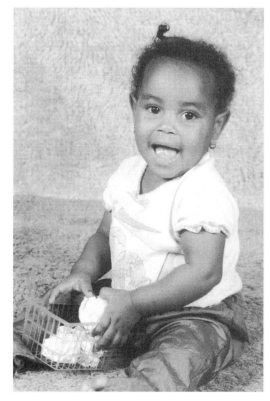

Catching a ball is more difficult than throwing one, and toddlers, for the most part, are not very good at it. Typically, a toddler will stand with his arms out while the ball bounces against his tummy. Parents who are interested in teaching their child to catch are best off starting with a large beach ball. Eventually, many parents become interested in teaching their child other kinds of ball games. They help their child learn to hit a ball with a baseball bat, a golf club, or a tennis racquet. For the time being, however, one-year-olds have their hands full just exploring the surprising assortment of balls that exist, from the incredible bounciness of a racquet ball to the slippery heaviness of a child-sized bowling ball.

PLAYING WITH BLOCKS AND BUILDING MATERIALS

In an earlier chapter, we talked about how children are interested in emptying things before they turn their attention to filling. We see this same sort of progression in block play. Long before toddlers show a spontaneous interest in building block towers, they obviously relish knocking them down. Actually the game of "build and crash" that children play with parents is an early experiment in balance. In this game, children recognize the instability of their parent's tower and take on the mischievous role of upsetting the balance. In other spontaneous games, which are not on so grand a scale, toddlers may take over the role of the balancer. A miniature cow is stood up on its legs, or a doll is balanced on the window sill.

Balance experiments with one-year-olds can be extended in at least two ways. For children who show an inclination to build higher, parents can demonstrate how a tower may be con-

structed in layers. Each layer consists of a pedestal with objects balanced on top of it. Large flat books and cookie sheets work well as the pedestals, while smaller blocks or margarine containers are placed between the layers. The same idea can work with large hard books and small tin cans. Place several cans on top of the book, then another book across the cans, more cans on top and another book, etc. The tower looks like a Dagwood sandwich, with books for slices of bread and tin cans as the fixings.

The second extension occurs when one-year-olds become interested in arranging a set of objects on top of a pedestal. One miniature doll on the arm of a chair is joined by the rest of the doll family, or one tomato juice can with one miniature car parked on top is transformed into a parking lot full of cars.

PLAYING WITH CARS AND TRUCKS

Cars and trucks of all sizes and varieties are among the most popular items in every toy store. The fascination with cars and trucks begins at a very early age. One of the most popular toys on the market is a child-size car with a door that opens and closes and a steering wheel that turns. As a toddler steps into this real-looking car, shuts the door, turns the key, and twirls the steering wheel, his intense expression tells us that, at least for the moment, he is in the driver's seat.

Although toddlers enjoy big vehicles they can scoot on, or steering wheels they can maneuver, miniature vehicles offer the greatest possibilities for parent-child play. Games with miniature vehicles spontaneously emerge as toddlers and parents push their vehicles along the floor, making "vrum vrum" noises. Sometimes these games are quite simple. Parents and toddlers drive their cars around the room, under the table, or along the edge of the sofa. Perhaps they experiment with a somewhat rougher terrain and drive their cars over each others' bodies. A driving game version of hide and seek may be played, with the parent driving in a circle around the child, now behind the child's back, now in front, bumping over the child's shoes, or shooting between the child's legs.

Another variation of car play is follow the leader. "Come on, follow me," the parent says to start the game. Then, as the parent drives in and around pieces of furniture and the child follows, the parent provides a running commentary: "Okay up the table leg... up (unh), up (unh) shift into low gear (irrhhRRR), now around the sugar bowl... no stopping for food... jump off the side (Yahhhh)!"

For parents and children interested in building, cars and trucks provide an obvious extension of block play. Blocks can be used to build simple garages or parking lots for favorite cars. Parents can help their one-year-old build short tunnels to drive cars through, or bridges over which the cars can drive. Blocks and plastic trays make great ramps and hills.

As your child becomes better able to understand imaginary play, you may want to introduce more elaborate themes related to vehicles. One theme might be called "taking care of the car." Toddlers notice that cars are constantly in need of more gas, more air, or some other kind of maintenance. Thomas, at eighteen months, was especially intrigued with drive-through car washes, and so it was quite natural for Thomas and his mother to go into the car-wash business. Using a shoebox, they created a tunnel for washing their collection of miniature vehicles. Systematically, Thomas gave each car a turn driving through the car wash. His mother maintained a pitch of excitement by taking on the role of announcer. "Here comes Thomas driving the Chevrolet! Up to the car wash he comes! Swish-swish-swish. On goes the water! Here come the soap suds! Off goes the water! Out comes the car!"

Children, like Thomas, who have a strong interest in real vehicles may respond to a variety of imaginary themes if stimulated by their parents. However, these pretend episodes with a one-year-old will usually remain very brief. Most of the time one-year-olds and their parents just tune into the movement of their toy vehicles. They are caught up in the way the rolling motion of the wheels is transferred to the hand of the would-be driver, the feel of the open road in a driving fantasy.

PLAYING WITH DOLLS

Whether a rag doll wears a face that is happy or sad, one's first impulse is to give it some love. The doll's big button eyes and stitched-on mouth bring out one's protective feelings. Parents naturally communicate this attitude to their one-year-old. Seeing a doll on the floor, they urge their one-year-old to pick it up and give it a reassuring hug.

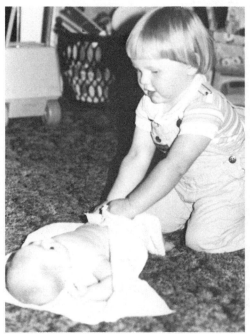

Indeed, parents can encourage their one-year-old to respond in a variety of ways to the presumed unhappiness of dolls and stuffed animals. A doll may be crying because it is hungry and needs to be fed, or because it is tired and wants to go to bed. Perhaps the crying means the doll is cold and should be wrapped in a blanket. Maybe the doll is simply upset and needs to be rocked in a rocking chair. Naturally these various responses to imagined distress are first modeled by parents (or older children), and then gradually adopted by one-year-olds.

Parents who choose to elaborate on the unhappiness of dolls and stuffed animals do so because they enjoy care-giving play with their children. These parents are oriented toward stimulating a child's sense of empathy and they feel good when they see their one-year-old pretending to be helpful and caring. The child may not be learning much about real care giving, but they are picking up the importance of empathizing with another person's discomfort.

Projecting aches and pains on a doll is only the starting point for encouraging nurturance. Parents who want to realize the potential of doll play can invest a doll or stuffed animal with positive feelings as well. Speaking for the doll, the parents can bring out these feelings. "Hi," a doll may greet the one-year-old in the morning. "Do you want to see me dance?" "Let's go take a bath," a doll may suggest. "I want to splash water." Dolls that converse, instead of just crying, become friends and companions, giving the one-year-old a chance to empathize with a wider range of emotions.

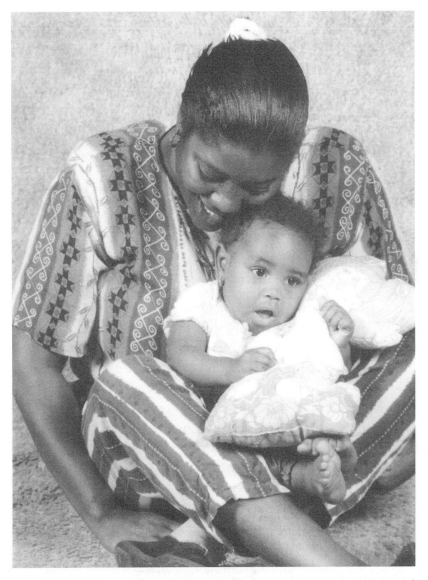

Over time, each doll and stuffed animal that is animated by parents acquires a unique personality. A large blue dragon becomes known as the "tickling dragon" because he specializes in wrestling with a one-year-old. A fat bear who is perpetually hungry joins the child at breakfast time. A doll with gymnastic tendencies regularly asks the child to catch her as she goes down the slide or jumps into the crib. This cast of characters enables parents to speak to their toddler in several voices, to offer adult guidance and suggestions in a variety of playful guises. More importantly, the child is surrounded by a group of friends. It is as if the charm of the "Sesame Street" characters has been drawn out of the television set and into the child's home.

Parents who encourage doll play find it has practical advantages too. Acting out a simplified sleep routine with a stuffed animal helps a one-year-old accept bedtime. Giving a baby doll a bottle of water instead of milk makes it easier for the one-year-old to accept a similar substitution. In time, doll play may even provide reassurance for a one-year-old. A child who gets in the habit of rocking an upset doll or putting a doll to sleep may use these play routines for comfort.

Parents can lay the groundwork for independent doll play by using simple props in their demonstrations. A receiving blanket for the doll's clothes, a cardboard box for a bed, a doll bottle for feeding; these are adequate accessories in the beginning. They are simple enough to be used by a one-year-old without adult assistance, when and if the child acts out imaginary themes on her own.

Ultimately the success of doll play depends upon children forming attachments to their dolls. Parents can point out that dolls are crying and they can give them personalities, but they cannot determine a child's feeling toward the dolls. A one-year-old may prefer stuffed animals to traditional dolls, or adopt a collection of miniature characters who can travel together in a bucket or bag. Imaginary babies and friends come in many forms, and children do not always select the ones that parents find most attractive.

In fact, when one-year-olds first start playing with dolls, their favorites often become distinctly less attractive. Out of curiosity, children pull off or poke out the doll's eyes. They twist off arms, legs, and heads. Parents can anticipate this mutilation and respond by fixing the dolls as much as possible in a kindly, matter-of-fact way. The children's behavior does not foreshadow a cruel nature. Quite likely by the time they are approaching the age of two, these same children will show special concern for the doll who is missing an eye or who has lost most of its hair.

Within the broad themes of caregiver play and friendship play, there are many different ways to pretend with dolls and stuffed toys. Parents can encourage doll play by treating the doll like a member of the family, providing it with clothes or a blanket and encouraging their child to bring their doll to the table. Parents can also talk for the doll or describe the way the doll is feeling. At first, your child might be an onlooker while you are playing with the doll. After a while he will join in or imitate the play. As your child plays with the doll, she is discovering a fundamental idea of pretending. It is exciting for parents to see this idea dawning in the minds of one-year-olds as they talk to their dolls and stuffed animals

PLAY IDEAS

Parents of one- to two-year-olds are likely to be as excited about a new toy as their youngster. Watching a toddler discover the potential of different types of toy play is a high point in parenting a toddler. In Play Ideas, we describe four different kinds of toy play: playing with balls, playing with blocks and building materials, playing with cars and trucks, and playing with dolls. Before buying a new toy for your toddler, observe your toddler's toy play. Choose from the suggestions we offer and the toys and activities that sustain your child's interest.

Playing With Balls

Fetch It

One of the earliest ways to play with a ball is a game of fetch. The parent rolls a ball across the floor and the toddler retrieves it. If your child is walking well, a basketball is ideal for this game because it is such a challenge to pick up and carry.

Catch It

As your child progresses to a game of catch, you will notice that her ability to throw far exceeds her ability to catch. You can solve this problem by handing your child a small ball, encouraging her to throw it to you, and then handing it back to her for another throw. This means that you and your child will be only three to five feet apart, which is just about the right range for a one-year-old's throwing skill.

Ball Choice

Inside ball games can be nerve-racking. However, there are a variety of balls that are satisfactory. Safe balls include paper balls, Ping-Pong balls, foam balls, rolled up socks, and balls of yarn. If your child is interested in learning to catch a ball, a balloon or beach ball works best. It moves slowly enough to be tracked and is relatively easy to trap against the chest. Of course, blowing up the ball is half the fun.

Golf and tennis balls are not very suitable for indoor play but their bounciness is intriguing. Dropping a golf ball on a path in the back yard and chasing it as it bounces is a game with endless variations for a toddler. Here a parent is playing an indoor game with the same kind of unpredictability. As the pan is tilted, the golf ball rolls back and forth around the outer edge just slowly enough to look like it can be caught by the child, just fast enough to be one step ahead of her outstretched hand.

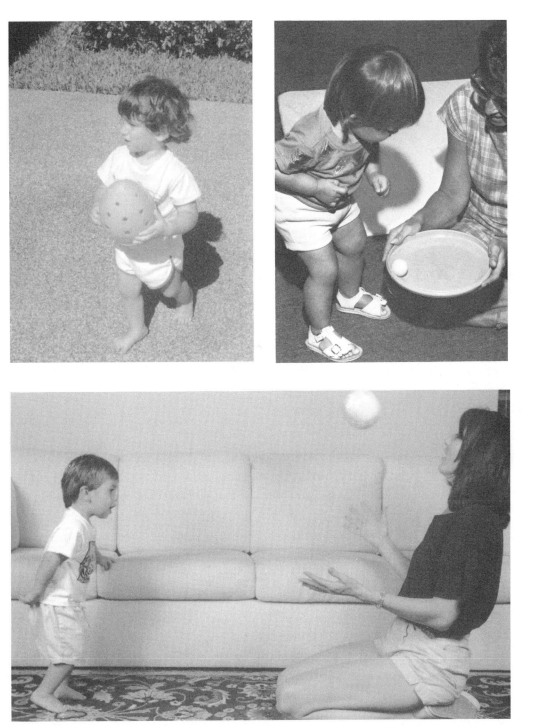

Playing With Blocks and Building Materials

Look-Out

When toddlers first show interest in tower building, they are most impressed with their ability to knock down towers. You can encourage your child to experiment with building towers by showing her how to balance a miniature doll or animal on top of the tower. As a lookout, the tower is likely to be left standing a little bit longer.

Building Blocks

Many toddlers are interested in stacking household objects. Small cereal boxes, toilet paper rolls, or margarine tubs make good building materials. Tin cans are very stable, especially full cans, although they may be too heavy for the child to handle safely. Empty tin cans with blunt edges can be made more appealing by decorating them with wrapping paper or wallpaper scraps.

High Rises

More complex towers can be built in layers. Build several short towers of the same height, and top them with a broad horizontal support, such as a book or cookie sheet. Construct addi-

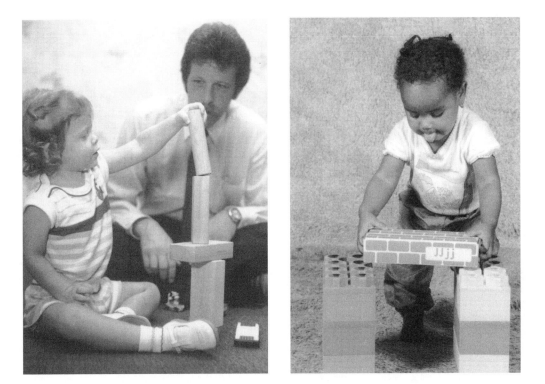

tional layers in the same way. This advanced type of tower is good for parents who enjoy building with their one-year-old.

Block Designs

It is easier to build flat constructions because the problem of balance does not need to be solved. Given a variety of interesting shapes and colors, your child may be interested in creating a design or enclosure. At first toddlers tend to combine only a few pieces, perhaps repeating their discovery a number of times. Gradually their ideas become more expansive. You may want to make an occasional suggestion, but this is a good opportunity for you to observe your child's awareness and interest in building original structures.

Line Up

One-year-olds who enjoy building are likely to explore the nature of a straight line. They may line up toy cars, animals, balls, virtually anything. You can introduce a game of fill the hole. Make a line with a set of objects, then move an object from the middle of the line to one end: "I think I'll move up here—chug-chug-chug." Wait to see if your child does anything to fill this hole in the middle of the line. If not, demonstrate a possible solution by moving a second object into the first hole. This creates a second hole. As you and your child fill old holes and make new ones, you will be putting together and taking apart the line. It is like building up and knocking down a tower, except that the line is not destroyed every time a hole is created in it.

Playing With Cars and Trucks

Dirt Dump

Dump trucks and pick up trucks make fine outdoor toys. With a small shovel, your child can fill up the trucks with sand or dirt and empty them out again. Don't be surprised if she ends up with more dirt on her clothes and in her shoes than in the trucks.

Follow the Lead Car

The kitchen table is a great surface for driving small vehicles. You and your toddler can maneuver your cars without crawling on the floor. Try a game of follow the leader. Encourage your child to follow your lead as you perform various stunts: driving around a plate, jumping the salt shaker, or hiding under a napkin.

Train Maker

Create a train by attaching two or three shoe boxes together. Your child will enjoy filling up the cars with different kinds of toys, animals, cars, play food, film cases, spools, or odd puzzle pieces. It is unlikely that a one-year-old will sort the toys according to category, but you may end up with an animal car or a car full of play food.

Blocks and Trucks

Playing with cars and trucks is more fun when you add some simple block structures. You can build a tunnel for cars to go through, a garage for parking, or a ramp for racing. In fact, all kinds of building stuff offers possibilities. Cars can be pushed through cardboard tubes, balanced on top of margarine containers, and raced down cookie sheet ramps.

Delivery Trucks

If you like to play with cars and trucks, you can introduce some pretend themes that will be novel for your one-year-old. Pretend you are fixing the cars, putting gasoline in them, or washing them. Or pretend you are taking a trip in a car or truck. A third idea is to use a toy dumptruck for deliveries. The truck might deliver popcorn, for example, to members of the family while they are watching television. Perhaps dirty socks can be transported to the clothes hamper.

Playing With Dolls

Doll Props

Not all toddlers are attracted to doll play. If your child is, you will find that simple props can stimulate independent play. A blanket works well for dressing the baby, a cardboard box makes a good crib, and a plastic baby bottle suffices for feeding. More elaborate props are not necessary, and they may cause frustration.

Hair Dresser

One-year-olds sometimes want to play out more advanced themes with their dolls. Any experience with strong emotional significance may be reenacted in doll play, especially if you participate in the play.

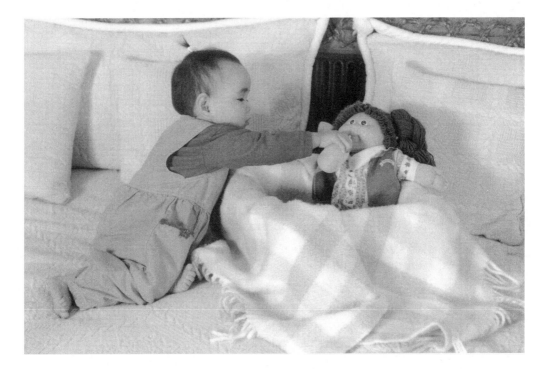

Doll Play

Dolls usually start out as babies, but soon they become peer friends as well. Your one-year-old may enjoy sharing a variety of experiences with this new friend. Together they may go down the slide, ride on the back of a bicycle, or take a bath in the tub.

Doll Talk

Dolls are very exciting companions when they talk. You can become the voice of a favorite doll or stuffed animal. The chance to interact with an animated doll will be seen as a special treat whether or not your one-year-old is talking much.

Miniatures

Many toddlers are attracted to miniature dolls. If your child likes to carry around several of these dolls, introduce a game of taking turns. The dolls might be jumping off the window ledge or riding in a toy bus. Whatever they are doing, there will be an opportunity for you to demonstrate the idea of taking turns: "Okay Bert. Now it's your turn to jump. Good! Now, Ernie, it's your turn. Everybody will get a chance."

Animal Stunts

Show your child ways to make a toy animal do tricks; jump, dance, slide down, climb up, run, stop, touch your toes, stand on your head.

Other Fun Activities With Toys

Scribble Away

Buy a box of jumbo crayons. Put sheets of paper on the floor and join your toddler in a scribble game. Of course, your toddler will not be able to draw a picture, but she'll be thrilled with the idea of making a mark. When the drawing is over, play a filling game to get the crayons back in the box.

Animal Dig

Most, but not all, toddlers love to dig. Place several miniature animals on the bottom of a large cardboard box and cover with loose soil. Let your toddler dig for the animals. (This is definitely an outdoor game.)

Animal Fun

Use a box top as a road and help your toddler make a parade of animals. Add to the fun by showing her how to make each animal jump in the box. Make sounds—a moo, an oink, or perhaps a quack—as each animal takes a turn.

Rock Band Drummer

If you can tolerate a little noise, a collection of pans and a wooden mixing spoon make a fine toy for an active toddler. Play a tape with a strong beat as your child beats the upside down pans. Add to the fun by giving your child pot lids that she can use as cymbals.

Piano Playing

Your toddler may enjoy a toy piano. Although you can't expect your toddler to play a tune, she is likely to discover ways of playing high or low notes or of making very soft and very loud noises. Ultimately she will discover the fun of banging all the notes with both fists at the same time.

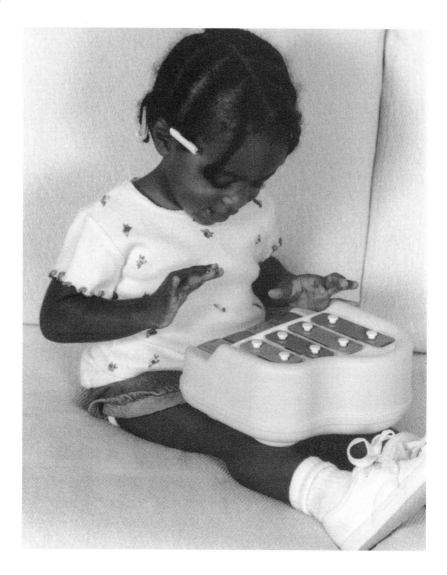

Toy Photo

Take a picture of your toddler's security toy and put it in a frame in his room. Saying goodnight to the photo of the toy can be a part of the night time routine. Put the frame away as soon as your toddler loses interest. When she is a little older, she will enjoy seeing a picture of the huggy she loved when she was a baby.

CHAPTER 13

Pretending

~~~~~~~~~~~~~~~~~~~~~~~~~~~~~~~~

Scene: Marcel, a one-year-old, is sitting on the floor banging pots and pans with a spoon.

Mother (bringing him his stuffed dog): "Doggie is hungry. Let's give him some supper." (She mimes feeding the dog with a wooden spoon.)

Marcel's father comes into the kitchen a few minutes later and sees Marcel bringing the spoon to the dog's mouth.

Father (in amazement): "Look at that! Marcel is pretending to feed his dog!"

Although Marcel's feat was probably imitation rather than true pretending, his father had a right to be excited. Just by watching his mother pretend to feed the dog, Marcel recognized a spoon goes into a mouth. During his second year, Marcel will continue to make connections between objects and how they are used. He will sweep when he sees a broom, bang when he sees a hammer, and try to put a sock on his foot.

Putting together objects that either belong or are used together is an important accomplishment that leads to genuine pretending. By the time he turns two, Marcel will put the spoon in the mouth of each of his animals in turn, even though he has never watched his mother feed his menagerie.

In this chapter we describe ways in which children make the transition from imitation to pretending: Playing Out a Familiar Theme, Going Out, Telephone Play, Going to the Doctor, Replaying a Recent Event, Animating Objects, Substituting a Play Object for a Real One, and Engaging in Early Role Play.

~~~

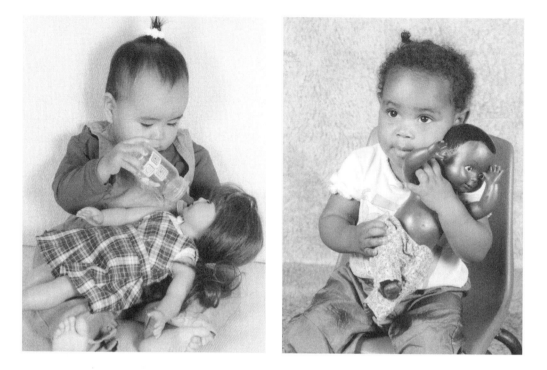

PLAYING OUT A FAMILIAR THEME

The Scene: A child-sized table with a play tea set on it.
Theresa: "Sit down, Daddy, chair."
Father: "Oh, dinner must be ready. I feel like some spaghetti. Could you cook me
some?"
Theresa: "Want psghetti Daddy?" (Theresa hands him an empty plate and a plastic
fork.)
Father: "Spaghetti—that's exactly what I want. But did you make enough for
Teddy? He wants a bite too."
Theresa (putting the spoon in the teddy bear's mouth): "Eat psghetti, Teddy."

In this play exchange with her father, Theresa played a secondary role. Her father made suggestions and she followed his lead. In a few months, as Theresa becomes more verbal, she will become an equal partner in a pretend play scenario.

Familiar themes that you may want to try out with your toddler include Going Out, Telephone Play, and Going to the Doctor.

Going Out

A play theme rich in conversational possibilities is going out. The most likely version is a shopping trip. For some time your toddler may have been interested in pushing a toy shopping cart around the house. From time to time, he may have tried on bits of adult apparel: a necklace, a pair of shoes, a hat. He may be putting these two routines together in a sensible way— he gets dressed up in adult garb in order to go shopping. But, although he looks ready to go, he probably does not have a clear idea why you are shopping or even where you are going. Your conversation can help to clarify matters, lengthen the play and make it more fun. You can suggest a logical

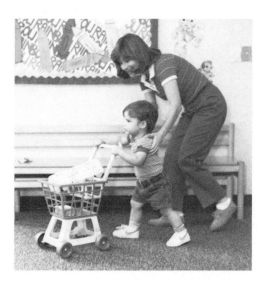

shopping place, "Are you going to Safeway?" or give a simple order, "Get me some pickles, please." You can hand the child play money to spend at the store, or offer a tongue-in-cheek piece of gratuitous advice, "Be careful crossing the streets."

The going out theme may appear in the form of going to work. Your child sits on a riding toy waves goodbye, and wheels out of the room. Again, you can elaborate the play with your comments, wishing your child a good day and reminding him to return home for supper. You might suggest an accessory such as a lunch box, a notebook, wallet, or sunglasses. Although outings to the beach, the park, or the mountains are relatively uncommon, an older toddler may collect a towel as if going swimming or show interest in a picnic cooler. You can respond by pretending that the child is going on a trip.

Telephone Play

The telephone is a familiar toy with obvious potential for conversational games. In the living room, a parent and one-year-old may place an imaginary phone call. "Whom shall we call?" the parent begins. "How about Uncle Jim?" After a brief conversation with Uncle Jim, the parent hands the telephone to her child and says. "He wants to talk to you." The child may shyly murmur "hi" and then "bye," or just silently hold the receiver

No matter, the parent takes the phone back and ends the conversation. Over time, a toddler will learn from these demonstrations and find a way to become more involved. Perhaps he will recite the names of other people in Uncle Jim's family, inviting his parent to talk to each one in turn. Maybe the child will designate with a word or two the topic of conversation. "Doggie" might mean tell Uncle Jim that we got a new dog, and "cwacker" might mean that Uncle Jim gives his a cracker when they go to his house.

You can also carry on conversations with your child using two phones. Since he needs to hold up one end of the conversation, these conversations tend to be brief and one-sided. You might begin, "Hello, do you want to go for a walk?" Your child nods his head. "You do? Get your shoes and we will go for a walk, bye-bye." Another way of carrying on a two-phoned conversation is for the parent to hold up a stuffed animal and pretend to talk for it. "Hello, I'm Harry, are you Keith?" The toddler nods yes and the parent continues. "I'm hungry. Will you get me some cereal?" Quite likely the child drops the telephone and runs into the kitchen to look for the cereal.

Going to the Doctor

Doctor play can help a one-year-old tolerate a visit to the doctor. Using a play or improvised doctor's kit you can prepare your toddler for a visit to the doctor, or to replay a visit that was traumatic. You might pick up the play otoscope from the doctor's kit and begin a pretend examination. "Let me look at your

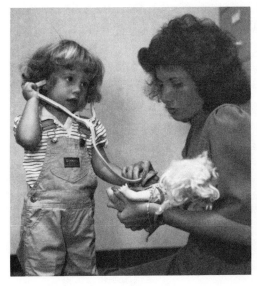

fingernails." (This will not threaten your child.) "Hmm, your fingernails are growing nicely." Moving up to your child's face you can then examine the tip of her nose. Then you can say quite casually, "Oh, I almost forgot to look in your ears. Does it tickle?" Such conversations may appear to be over your child's head, but they might help your toddler deal with the intrusiveness of a physical examination. In the same way, you can pretend to look into your child's mouth, take his temperature, or check his heart-beat.

With little or no encouragement your older toddler may take on the role of doctor with either you or a doll assuming the role of patient. As the patient, you can ask your child to put a bandage on your finger or give you a shot in your arm. Then you can say to your child, "That only hurt for a tiny second. You are a good doctor."

Doctor play, like the other pretend themes we have discussed in this chapter, involves complicated ideas for a one-year-old. Sometimes your child will watch you play out a scene without making any effort to participate. In fact, you may feel you are playing virtually by yourself. Eventually however, your child will pick up the idea and join in. Through words or gestures, he will choose a role that pleases him and a pretend game will emerge where both you and your child play active roles.

The play themes that we have described are the most common, but certainly not the only themes that you play out with your child. Theme play is most successful if you play out a theme that is especially familiar or recent. A trip to the shoe store can lead to a pretend game with Daddy's shoes. If your child is the salesman, ask him to try on several pairs of shoes. The first pair can be too big, the second too small, the third a yucky color, and the fourth just right.

Other themes that you might try out are wrapping up packages, playing football games, packing up for a trip, building a snowman, going to a filling station, or visiting a relative. At first your toddler will play a minor role in your pretend theme, but in a surprisingly short time he will get into the act and make his own contributions.

REPLAYING A RECENT EVENT

Lisa went to the barbershop with her father. She watched silently but intently as the barber took out the scissors and proceeded to cut her father's hair. In the middle of the haircut, Lisa got down on the floor, picked up some pieces of hair, and handed them to her father. When the barber continued the hair cutting, Lisa burst into tears and sniffled all the way home.

That evening, Lisa's father got out a pair of play scissors and a paper napkin. He wrapped the paper napkin around a Teddy Bear's neck and pretended to cut his hair. He then gave the play scissors to his daughter. Lisa took the scissors, placed them near the Teddy Bear's head, and then looked on the floor for cut-off hair. By the time Lisa's mother came home, father and daughter were playing happily together.

Replaying a recent event that was scary and traumatic gives toddlers an opportunity to play out their fears and gain a sense of control. On the other hand, replaying a pleasant event gives toddlers a way of savoring the experience. The day after Lisa's ill-fated trip to the barber shop, Lisa and her father went to the zoo together. Later in the day, Lisa's Teddy Bear had a fine opportunity to taste a banana and three crackers.

ANIMATING OBJECTS

Alberto was sitting on the floor playing with a basket of miniature animals. For quite a while he amused himself by taking the animals out of the basket and putting them back in. Then, as his mother looked on, he took a cow out of the basket, made a "moo" noise, and hopped the cow along the floor. On another day he picked out the dog and the lion, and gave each animal a turn to hop along the floor, making "woofing" and "roaring" noises.

Like imitation, animating objects provides a foundation for pretending. In another year or so, Alberto is likely to create a play landscape, lining up cows and offering them hay, or engaging two cars in a race across the floor. He may also treat his stuffed lion like a baby, wrapping it in a blanket, putting it to sleep, offering it a bottle, and burping it over his shoulder.

SUBSTITUTING A PLAY OBJECT FOR A REAL ONE

Pedro loved to go to McDonalds. Early one morning his mother saw him taking some crayons out of a bag and putting them in his mouth. "What are you doing?" she asked. "Eat 'appy meal," Pedro explained.

Paulette went to the pet store with her parents and watched the pet store owner give the puppies biscuits. When she came home she picked up her stuffed lion and gave it a bit of her block.

Children like Pedro and Paulette who substitute one object for another have made an important discovery. They realize that a prop can be two things at the same time: a crayon can be a french fried potato and still be a crayon; a block can be a lion's dinner and still be a block. This emerging ability to use one object to represent another foreshadows the onset of pretend play.

ENGAGING IN EARLY ROLE PLAY

Danny had been playing on the kitchen floor banging pot lids together. His mother was getting ready for guests. Positive that Danny had grown out of the destructive stage, she placed a vase of glass flowers on the coffee table, and left the room. When she returned, there was Danny squatting at the coffee table pouring a cup of orange juice on the glass flowers. "What on earth are you doing!?" his mother asked in a state of shock. "Flowers thirsty," Danny responded, as he continued to pour in the juice.

When pretending first emerges, whether the toddler is watering glass flowers, mooing like a cow, or dressing up in his mother's shoes, it is difficult to know whether he has really grasped the

concept of role playing. Was Danny pretending to be in charge of watering thirsty flowers, or did he decide that watering the flowers with orange juice was a fun idea? It is quite likely that both explanations are true. Danny acted out the role of "flower waterer" knowing perfectly well that the flowers were only pretend. However, once he began to water them they became real in his mind, and he watered them in earnest.

Although full-fledged pretending, where your child joins with another child in inventing a story line and acting out a theme, does not emerge until your child is two or three, the foundation for pretending is laid in the toddler year. As you play imaginatively with your child, you are helping him make the transition from imitation to pretending.

PLAY IDEAS

We have talked throughout the chapter about the fine line between imitation and pretending. For the most part, one-year-olds are imitating an adult when they play out a familiar theme, replay a recent event, animate an object, or play a familiar role. However, children under two years old, with a playful adult as their model, may begin to make the transition between imita-

tion and pretend play. In this section we present some play ideas that will spark your child's imagination and encourage early pretending. Select ideas that are appropriate for your child. Don't be concerned if your child watches your pretending and doesn't join in. Just as you observe your child closely before you initiate play ideas, your child needs to watch you for a while before he can join in your play.

Playing Out A Familiar Theme

Making Dinner

Cooking, serving, and eating are everyday events for all children. It is therefore logical that toddlers' early attempts to play out a theme would be related to food. For some children, cooking is a large part of making dinner and their favorite pretend

theme is mixing something in a bowl or putting a pot on a play stove. Other children are more interested in serving and eating. They enjoy putting play food on a dish and pretending to serve it or eat it. Because eating is a social experience, a food theme is more likely to emerge when an adult is there to join in. If your child enjoys being the chef, select props that are associated with cooking: a plastic mixing bowl, an eggbeater, a large spoon, and a strainer. If your child prefers serving or eating, choose props associated with eating: paper or plastic plates, plastic spoons, napkins, play foods, and three placemats (one for your child, one for you, and one for a guest doll or teddy).

Sports

Whether or not you and your spouse are interested in sports, most children, by the time they are two, have watched a sport on television. Because most sports involve playing ball, and your child has enjoyed ball play since he was quite small, he is likely to put sport props to immediate use. Suggestions for sport props include a soft ball and bat, a baseball cap, and a sports jersey.

Shopping

Your child may have both good and bad associations with shopping. Shopping in a toy store or shoe store is likely to be associated with having a good time. Shopping in a crowded mall is likely to be associated with looking at a whole lot of legs or waiting endlessly at a checkout counter. A collection of appro-priate shopping props gives your child an opportunity to play out a shopping theme the way he would like it to be. Suggestions for shopping props: purses, wallets, play money, fake credit cards, and a set of keys.

Holidays

Holidays create happy memories for toddlers. You can keep these memories alive by encouraging your toddler to replay a holiday that your family has celebrated. When you gather props for the holiday theme, make sure not to overwhelm your toddler with too many props. Three to four props is all you need to inspire your child to play out a celebration. Here are some suggestions for some of the holidays. Choose props that your child is familiar with for whatever holiday you select.

Suggestions for Halloween props: masks that are not scary, trick or treat bags, play apples, empty candy boxes, and Halloween decorations.

Suggestions for birthday props: candles, modeling clay (to make a cake), pretend presents, party blowers, hats, and loot bags.

Suggestions for Fourth of July props: flag, noisemakers, a picnic basket, a flashlight, and red, white, and blue paper napkins.

Replaying a Recent Event

Replaying a recent event is somewhat different from playing out a theme. When you and your child have shared a happy experience, you both will enjoy recalling and replaying the experience. At the same time, replaying an experience that was scary or unpleasant for your child can make it easier for your child to cope.

Birthday Party

Toddlers are likely to feel ambiguous about a birthday party. Eating cake and ice cream and receiving a goody bag may delight your child, while being immersed in a crowd of people including many strangers can be somewhat overwhelming. Select props that will help you remember the fun parts of the party. Suggestions for birthday party props: sand or clay to make a cake, candles, balloons, paper hats, and goody bags.

Visit to the Doctor

Even the most easygoing toddler may not enjoy a visit to the doctor. Replay the visit using a toy doctor's kit.

Thunderstorm

Many toddlers are scared of thunder and lightening. You can lessen your toddler's fear by letting him create his own version of a thunderstorm. Suggestions for thunderstorm props: flashlight, pie tins, and a cuddly doll or stuffed animal.

Animating a Toy

Small props like miniature cars or animals give your child an early opportunity to create a play landscape. At first, your child will simply manipulate the props, grouping together cars and animals that look alike, or lining them up in a row. If you take the lead in creating a scene and animating the props, your child will watch you intently and perhaps join in the play.

Animating a Play Car

Push a car across the floor making a "vrum, vrum" sound and pretend to fill it with gas. Give the car to your child and see if he joins the play.

Animating a Familiar Animal

Find a few animals that your child is familiar with. Feed each animal in turn, barking, mooing, or quacking, or whatever sound is appropriate. Give your toddler a turn.

Animating a Stuffed Animal or Doll

Pretend your child's doll or stuffed animal is real. Talk to it, pretend to feed it, brush its hair or teeth, and sing it to sleep.

Substituting a Play Object for a Real One

The substitution of a play object for a real one is an important intellectual feat. When your toddlers fills a cake pan with sand and calls it a birthday cake or puts a strainer on his head as if it is a hat, he is taking a beginning step toward abstract thinking. He has identified salient features of a cake and a hat and has identified play objects that share these features. A cake is soft and round and so is the sand in a cake pan. A hat is round and fits on his head just like a strainer.

Mailbox Play

Find an empty tissue box and use it like a mailbox. Fill the tissue box with some junk mail and let your child retrieve it. Next, give your child a turn putting the junk mail into the mailbox and talk about what he is doing.

Barn Play

Find an empty shoe box and cut one end off to make a door. Put several of your child's farm animals through the door into the barn. Say out loud, "OK, cow, go into the barn." Give your child a turn taking the animals out of the barn and making them go back in.

Tunnel Play

Find a spindle from a paper towel or gift wrap roll. Select two or three small cars or trucks and put them in one end of the spindle. Lift the end of the spindle and let the cars roll out of the other end. Say out loud, "OK, cars, here we go through the tunnel." Then give your child a turn putting the cars in the tunnel and letting them roll out.

Engaging in Early Role Play

Genuine role play, when a child pretends that he is someone else, is not likely to emerge before your child is two or three years old. The toddler who shampoos the duck's head in the

bath or struts around the house in his mother's shoes is likely to be imitating his parent rather than pretending that he is a parent. This distinction is evident when we watch two or three preschool children pretending. One child is apt to say to another, "You be the baby and I be your daddy." He is letting his friends know that he will take the part of father whatever props are available and however the "baby" behaves. Although toddlers are not ready to engage in this kind of sophisticated play, you can lay the groundwork for role-playing by playing a role while your child looks on, giving your child a pile of dress-up clothes, or engaging your child in a pretend conversation.

Parent as Pretender

For many toddlers their first introduction to role-playing is when they watch their parent take on a role. Make sure that the role you assume is familiar to your child.

Animal Pretending

Pretend you are a dog, cow, or zoo animal. Tell your child who you are pretending to be and see if he joins the game.

Visitor Pretending

Pretend you are another member of the family, your spouse, a grandmother, or perhaps another child. Make sure to tell your child who you are pretending to be. Make the role ring true for the child both by what you wear and what you do. Here are some examples:

Playing Grandfather

Put on a jacket or a pair of glasses that make you look like Grandpa. Talk to your child in a deep voice using words and actions that he would associate with grandfather. "Give me a high-five." "How about a hug for grandpa?" "I'm going to eat you up!"

Playing Fix-It Man

Put a few "safe" tools in a tool box. Announce that you are the fix-it man. "Do you have anything for me to fix? Oh, your truck wheel is lose? I'll fix it." Pretend to tighten the wheel with a screwdriver. "All fixed. Would you like a turn?"

Playing a Television Character

"I'm a clown. I'm wearing a clown hat. Let's sing a song. We're a happy family."

Dress-Up Play

At one time or other toddlers are likely to appear on the scene wearing some rather unusual outfits. At this age your toddler may not be pretending to be a Mother or Dad or getting ready

for an excursion, but it is a first step toward playing a role. Encourage your toddler to dress up by providing appropriate props. For a toddler, two or three props are more than sufficient.

- Dressing Up Like Mommy Props: necklace, scarf, jersey, purse, slippers.
- Dressing Up Like Daddy Props: tie, t-shirt, belt, shoes.
- Dressing Up for a Rainy Day Props: raincoat, rain hat, boots, child-size umbrella.
- Getting Ready to go to the Beach Props: towel, pail, shovel, robe, empty bottle of suntan lotion.
- Taking the Dog for a Walk Props: stuffed animal, leash, cracker.

Pretend Conversations

Pretend conversations provide a special opportunity for helping children learn to play a role. In the beginning you will introduce and sustain the conversation, but after a while your child will join in.

Doctor–Patient Conversations

Props: a toy otoscope and a toy hypodermic needle.

Pretend you are the patient and your child is the doctor. "Doctor," (use the child's name) "will you please look in my ears? I think there may be a frog in my left ear. No frog? Then I must have a bug in my ear. Could you please give me a shot?"

Shoe Store Salesman–Customer Conversation

Props: two pairs of shoes, a shoe box, and play money.

Pretend you are the customer and your child is the salesman. "I need new shoes. Do you have a pair that will fit me? No, that's no good. It hurts my little toe. Do you have another pair? Great, this pair fits fine. I think I will buy them. Do you need some money?"

Index

About the Author

MARILYN SEGAL, PH.D., the noted developmental psychologist, educator and researcher specializing in early childhood, is the founder and dean emeritus of the Nova Family and School Center and a tireless advocate on the national, state, and local level. The mother of five children, she has written 19 books, including the *Your Child at Play* series, *In Time and With Love*, *Making Friends*, and *Just Pretending*. She also produced a nine-part, public-service TV series *To Reach a Child*. She lives in Hollywood, Florida.

WENDY MASI, PH.D., continues in her mother Dr. Marilyn Segal's footsteps as a specialist in early childhood development. Currently the director of the Nova Family Center, she earned her Ph.D. in developmental psychology from Nova Southeastern University, where she initiated the parent-child program. Dr. Masi has devoted her professional activities to designing and implementing programs for families with young children, and frequently presents a wide variety of workshops and training programs based on the Family Center's work. She lives in Fort Lauderdale, Florida.

PARENTING/CHILDCARE BOOKS FROM NEWMARKET PRESS

Ask for these titles at your local bookstore or use this coupon and enclose a check or money order payable to: **Newmarket Press**, 18 East 48th Street, New York, NY 10017.

Amelia D. Auckett
Baby Massage
____ $12.95 pb (978-1-55704-022-0)

**Elissa P. Benedek, M.D., and
Catherine F. Brown, M.Ed.**
How to Help Your Child Overcome Your Divorce
____ $16.95 pb (978-1-55704-461-7)

Lucy Burney
Boost Your Child's Immune System
____ $14.95 pb (978-1-55704-642-0)

Sarah Cheyette, M.D.
Mommy, My Head Hurts: A Doctor's Guide to Your Child's Headaches
____ $22.95 hc (978-1-55704-471-6)
____ $12.95 pb (978-1-55704-535-5)

Anne Ford
Laughing Allegra
____ $24.95 hc (978-1-55704-564-5)
____ $16.95 pb (978-1-55704-622-2)
On Their Own
____ $24.95 hc (978-1-55704-759-5)
____ $16.95 pb (978-1-55704-725-0)

Lee F. Gruzen
Raising Your Jewish/Christian Child
____ $16.95 pb (978-1-55704-414-3)

Debra W. Haffner
Beyond The Big Talk: A Parent's Guide to Raising Sexually Healthy Teens
____ $24.95 hc (978-1-55704-472-3)
____ $16.95 pb (978-1-55704-811-0)
From Diapers to Dating: A Parent's Guide to Raising Sexually Healthy Children
____ $23.95 hc (978-1-55704-385-6)
____ $14.95 pb (978-1-55704-810-3)

What Every 21st-Century Parent Needs to Know: Facing Today's Challenges with Wisdom and Heart
____ $24.95 hc (978-1-55704-787-8)
____ $16.95 pb (978-1-55704-726-7)

Frederick Leboyer, M.D.
Inner Beauty, Inner Light: Yoga for Pregnant Women
____ $18.95 pb (978-1-55704-315-3)
Loving Hands: The Traditional Art of Baby Massage
____ $18.95 pb (978-1-55704-314-6)

Lynda Madaras & Area Madaras
Ready, Set, Grow!
____ $22.00 hc (978-1-55704-587-4)
____ $12.00 pb (978-1-55704-565-2)
On Your Mark, Get Set, Grow!
____ $22.00 hc (978-1-55704-780-9)
____ $12.00 pb (978-1-55704-781-6)
My Body, My Self for Boys
____ $12.95 pb (978-1-55704-767-0)
My Body, My Self for Girls
____ $12.95 pb (978-1-55704-766-3)
My Feelings, My Self
____ $12.95 pb (978-1-55704-442-6)
The "What's Happening to My Body?" Book for Boys
____ $24.95 hc (978-1-55704-769-4)
____ $12.95 pb (978-1-55704-765-6)
The "What's Happening to My Body?" Book for Girls
____ $24.95 hc (978-1-55704-768-7)
____ $12.95 pb (978-1-55704-764-9)

Sally Placksin
Mothering the New Mother, Rev. Ed.
____ $18.95 pb (978-1-55704-317-7)

Teresa Savage
The Ready-to-Read, Ready-to-Count Handbook
____ $16.95 pb (978-1-55704-413-6)

Dan Schaefer & Christine Lyons
How Do We Tell the Children? Third Ed.
____ $14.95 pb (978-1-55704-425-9)

Robert Schwebel, Ph.D.
Keep Your Kids Tobacco-Free
____ $14.95 pb (978-1-55704-369-6)
Saying No Is Not Enough, Rev. Ed.
____ $14.95 pb (978-1-55704-318-4)

Marilyn Segal, Ph.D.
In Time and With Love, 2nd Ed.
____ $18.95 pb (978-1-55704-445-7)
Your Child at Play: Birth to One Year, 2nd Ed.
____ $27.95 hc (978-1-55704-334-4)
____ $18.95 pb (978-1-55704-330-6)
Your Child at Play: One to Two Years, 2nd Ed.
____ $27.95 hc (978-1-55704-335-1)
____ $18.95 pb (978-1-55704-331-3)
Your Child at Play: Two to Three Years, 2nd Ed.
____ $27.95 hc (978-1-55704-336-8)
____ $18.95 pb (978-1-55704-332-0)
Your Child at Play: Three to Five Years, 2nd Ed.
____ $27.95 hc (978-1-55704-337-5)
____ $16.95 pb (978-1-55704-333-7)
Your Child at Play: Five to Eight Years
____ $29.95 hc (978-1-55704-402-0)
____ $17.95 pb (978-1-55704-401-3)

Eric Small
Kids & Sports
____ $14.95 pb (978-1-55704-532-4)
____ $24.95 hc (978-1-55704-498-3)

For postage and handling, please add $5.00 for the first book, plus $1.50 for each additional book. NY State residents, add applicable sales tax. Prices and availability are subject to change. Please allow 4–6 weeks for delivery.

I enclose a check or money order payable to **Newmarket Press** in the amount of $_____

Name _____

Address _____

City/State/Zip _____

For discounts on orders of five or more copies or to request a catalog, contact Newmarket Press, Special Sales Department, 18 East 48th Street, New York, NY 10017; phone 212-832-3575 or 800-669-3903; fax 212-832-3629; or e-mail sales@newmarketpress.com. **www.newmarketpress.com**